BOOKS BY BILL HYBELS

TOO BUSY
NOT
TO PRAY

Slowing down to be with God

BILL HYBELS
with LaVonne Neff

Including Questions for
Reflection and Discussion

InterVarsity Press
Downers Grove, Illinois

InterVarsity Press
P.O. Box 1400, Downers Grove, IL 60515, USA
World Wide Web: www.ivpress.com
E-mail: mail@ivpress.com

Second edition ©1998 by Bill Hybels.
First edition ©1988 by Bill Hybels.

InterVarsity Press® is the book-publishing division of InterVarsity Christian Fellowship/USA®, a student movement active on campus at hundreds of universities, colleges and schools of nursing in the United States of America, and a member movement of the International Fellowship of Evangelical Students. For information about local and regional activities, write Public Relations Dept., InterVarsity Christian Fellowship/USA, 6400 Schroeder Rd., P.O. Box 7895, Madison, WI 53707-7895.

All Scripture quotations, unless otherwise indicated, are taken from the Holy Bible, New International Version®. NIV®. *Copyright ©1973, 1978, 1984 by International Bible Society. Used by permission of Zondervan Publishing House. All rights reserved.*

Cover illustration: Comstock, Inc.

ISBN 0-8308-1972-X (cloth)
ISBN 0-8308-1971-1 (pbk.)

Printed in the United States of America ∞

Library of Congress Cataloging-in-Publication Data

Hybels, Bill.
    Too busy not to pray : slowing down to be with God : including
questions for reflection and discussion / Bill Hybels. — 2nd ed.,
10th anniversary ed. rev. & expanded.
        p. cm.
    ISBN 0-8308-1972-X (cloth). — ISBN 0-8308-1971-1 (paper)
    1. Prayer. I. Title.
BV210.2.H93 1998
248.3'2—dc21   *97-43784*
                                                                            CIP

21	20	19	18	17	16	15	14	13	12	11	10	9	8	7	6	5	4	3	2	1
16	15	14	13	12	11	10	09	08	07	06	05	04	03	02	01	00	99	98		

To Joel Jager:
a lifetime friend

1
God's Presence, God's Power

Prayer is an unnatural activity.

From birth we have been learning the rules of self-reliance as we strain and struggle to achieve self-sufficiency. Prayer flies in the face of those deep-seated values. It is an assault on human autonomy, an indictment of independent living. To people in the fast lane, determined to make it on their own, prayer is an embarrassing interruption.

Prayer is alien to our proud human nature. And yet somewhere, someplace, probably all of us reach the point of falling to our knees, bowing our heads, fixing our attention on God and praying. We may look both ways to be sure no one is watching; we may blush; but in spite of the foreignness of the activity, we pray.

Why are we drawn to prayer? I see two possible explanations.

Surrounded by God's Presence

We pray because, by intuition or experience, we understand

that *the most intimate communion with God comes only through prayer.*

Ask people who have faced tragedy or trial, heartbreak or grief, failure or defeat, loneliness or discrimination. Ask what happened in their souls when they finally fell on their knees and poured out their hearts to the Lord.

Such people have told me, "I can't explain it, but I felt like God understood me."

Others have said, "I felt surrounded by his presence."

Or, "I felt a comfort and peace I'd never felt before."

The apostle Paul knew this experience. Writing to the Christians at Philippi he said, "Do not be anxious about anything, but in everything, by prayer and petition, with thanksgiving, present your requests to God. And the peace of God, which transcends all understanding, will guard your hearts and your minds in Christ Jesus" (Philippians 4:6-7).

Several years ago my father, still a relatively young man and extremely active, died of a heart attack. As I drove to my mother's house in Michigan, I wondered how I would continue to function without the person who believed in me more than anyone else ever has or ever will.

That night in bed, I wrestled with God. "Why did this happen? How can I put it all together in my mind and in my life? Am I going to recover from losing my father? If you really love me, how could you do this to me?"

Suddenly, in the middle of the night, everything changed. It was as if I had turned a corner and was now facing a new direction. God simply said, "I'm able. I'm enough for you. Right now you doubt this, but trust me."

That experience may sound unreal, but its results were unmistakable. After that tear-filled, despairing night, I was never again tortured by doubt—either about God's care for me or about my ability to handle life without Dad. Grief, yes—his death wounded me deeply, and I will always miss him. But it did not set me adrift without anchor or compass. In the middle of the bleakest night I have ever known, one overpoweringly intimate moment with God gave me courage, reassurance and hope.

An Intimate Relationship

Prayer has not always been my strong suit. For many years, even as senior pastor of a large church, I *knew* more about prayer than I ever *practiced* in my own life. I have a racehorse temperament, and the tugs of self-sufficiency and self-reliance are very real to me. I didn't want to get off the fast track long enough to find out what prayer is all about.

But the Holy Spirit gave me a leading so direct that I couldn't ignore it, argue against it or disobey it. The leading was to explore, study and practice prayer until I finally understood it. I obeyed that leading. I read fifteen or twenty major books on prayer, some old and some new. I studied almost every passage on prayer in the Bible.

And then I did something absolutely radical: I prayed.

It has been twenty years since I began taking time to pray, and my prayer life has been transformed. The greatest fulfillment has not been the list of miraculous answers to prayers I have received, although that has been wonderful. The greatest thrill has been the qualitative difference in my relationship with God. And when I started to pray, I didn't know that was going to happen.

God and I used to be rather casually related to one another. We didn't get together and talk very much. Now, however, we get together a lot, not talking on the run but carrying on substantial, soul-searching conversations every morning for a good chunk of time. I feel as if I've gotten to know God a lot better since I started praying.

If the Holy Spirit is leading you to learn more about prayer, you are about to embark on a wonderful adventure. As you grow in prayer, God will reveal more of himself to you, breathing more of his life into your spirit. Mark my words, that will be the most fulfilling and rewarding part of your experience with prayer, more so even than the answers to prayer you are sure to receive. Fellowship with God, trust, confidence, peace, relief—these wonderful feelings will be yours as you learn how to pray.

A Channel for God's Power

Through prayer God gives us his peace, and that is one reason even self-sufficient people fall on their knees and pour out their hearts to him. But there is another reason. People are drawn to prayer because they know that *God's power* flows primarily to people who pray.

The Scriptures overflow with passages teaching that our almighty, omnipotent God is ready, willing and able to answer the prayers of his followers. The miracles of Israel's exodus from Egypt and journey to the Promised Land were all answers to prayer. So were Jesus' miracles of stilling storms, providing food, healing the sick and raising the dead. As the early church formed and grew and spread throughout the world, God answered the believers' continual prayers for healing and deliverance.

God's power can change circumstances and relationships. It can help us face life's daily struggles. It can heal psychological and physical problems, remove marriage obstructions, meet financial needs—in fact, it can handle any kind of difficulty, dilemma or discouragement.

Someone has said that when we work, *we* work; but when we pray, *God* works. His supernatural strength is available to praying people who are convinced to the core of their beings that he can make a difference. Skeptics may argue that answered prayers are only coincidences, but as an English archbishop once observed, "It's amazing how many coincidences occur when one begins to pray."

Hands Raised to Heaven

A story in the Old Testament has persuaded me more than any other biblical passage that prayer has significant results. It is found in Exodus 17:8-13:

> The Amalekites came and attacked the Israelites at Rephidim. Moses said to Joshua, "Choose some of our men and go out to fight the Amalekites. Tomorrow I will stand on top of the hill with the staff of God in my hands."
>
> So Joshua fought the Amalekites as Moses had ordered, and Moses, Aaron and Hur went to the top of the hill. As long as Moses held up his hands, the Israelites were winning, but whenever he lowered his hands, the Amalekites were winning. When Moses' hands grew tired, they took a stone and put it under him and he sat on it. Aaron and Hur held his hands up—one on one side,

one on the other — so that his hands remained steady till sunset. So Joshua overcame the Amalekite army with the sword.

Moses, Israel's famous leader, is faced with a crisis. An enemy army has just arrived near Israel's desert camp intent on wiping out Israel.

Moses calls in his most capable military leader for a discussion of military strategy. After a thorough planning session, Moses announces the approach they will take. "Joshua," he says, "tomorrow you take the best fighting men we have; lead them out on the plains to meet the enemy; and fight with courage. I am going to take two men with me, climb the hill that overlooks the plains and raise my hands toward heaven. I'm going to pray that God will pour out courage, valor, coordination and supernatural protection on our troops. Then I'm going to watch and see what God does."

God's Power Released

Joshua agrees. He believes in prayer, and he would rather have Moses' prayer support than his military support. What happens, of course, is that when Moses' hands are stretched heavenward, Joshua's troops prevail in battle, fighting with a divine intensity that drives back the enemy.

But, as can be expected, Moses' arms grow weary. He drops them to his sides and walks around the hill, viewing the battle. To his horror, the tide of battle shifts right before his eyes. Joshua's troops are being struck down; the enemy is gaining a toehold.

Moses stretches his arms toward heaven again and brings

the matter to the Lord. Immediately the battle's momentum shifts back to Joshua and the Israelites, and once again they are driving the enemy back. And then it strikes Moses. He must keep his arms stretched toward heaven in prayer if he wants to open the door for God's supernatural intervention on the battlefield.

Moses discovered that day that God's prevailing power is released through prayer. When I began praying in earnest, I discovered the same thing. It boils down to this: if you are willing to invite God to involve himself in your daily challenges, you will experience his prevailing power—in your home, in your relationships, in the marketplace, in the schools, in the church, wherever it is most needed.

That power may come in the form of wisdom—an idea you desperately need and can't come up with yourself. It may come in the form of courage greater than you could ever muster. It may come in the form of confidence or perseverance, uncommon staying power, a changed attitude toward a spouse or a child or a parent, changed circumstances, maybe even outright miracles. However it comes, God's prevailing power is released in the lives of people who pray.

Keep the Power Flowing

The other side of that equation is sobering: it is hard for God to release his power in your life when you put your hands in your pockets and say, "I can handle it on my own." If you do that, don't be surprised if one day you get the nagging feeling that the tide of battle has shifted against you and that you're fairly powerless to do anything about it.

Prayerless people cut themselves off from God's prevailing power, and the frequent result is the familiar feeling of being overwhelmed, overrun, beaten down, pushed around, defeated. Surprising numbers of people are willing to settle for lives like that. Don't be one of them. Nobody has to live like that. *Prayer is the key to unlocking God's prevailing power in your life.*

Once Moses made the connection between prayer and God's power, he determined to spend the rest of the day praying for God's involvement in the battle. But his arms grew weary. He knew better than to drop them to his sides; he had done that and watched his troops get wiped out. So the two men who accompanied him up the hill found a stone he could sit on. Then each man crawled under an arm and helped Moses hold his arms up. What a picture — Moses being supported by caring people who wanted to help him keep the power flowing! Needless to say, Israel won the battle that day.

Are you weary of praying? Do you feel that your prayers are ineffective? Do you wonder if God is really listening? In this book I'd like to play the role of one of Moses' friends, helping you hold up your arms until the day is done and the victory is yours. I'd like to be used by God to inspire you to continue to pray no matter how discouraged you may feel right now.

I know that God answers prayer. He answers mine, and he will answer yours too. Furthermore, he *wants* to hear from you. Your adventure of prayer begins with his willingness to listen.

2

God Is Willing

☐ **God is busy keeping the cosmos in order. He doesn't** want to hear about my little problems.

☐ God would think I was selfish if I prayed for my own needs. If I really love him, I'll put myself in last place.

☐ I know that "the cattle on a thousand hills" belong to God, but that's just a figure of speech. He's not in the business of taking care of me, and I won't ask him to do it.

Have you ever made any statements like these? If so, you're not alone, but you're tragically mistaken. Those statements are all based on a lie straight from hell—the lie that God doesn't care about his children.

Jesus told his disciples a story to help them understand how God feels about our prayers. Unfortunately, many people misunderstand the story. In fact, some Christians think it says just the opposite of what Jesus intended.

The story is recorded in Luke 18:2-5:

In a certain town there was a judge who neither feared

God nor cared about men. And there was a widow in that town who kept coming to him with the plea, "Grant me justice against my adversary." For some time he refused. But finally he said to himself, "Even though I don't fear God or care about men, yet because this widow keeps bothering me, I will see that she gets justice, so that she won't eventually wear me out with her coming!"

The Desperate Widow

The main character in the story is a widow. Of course it's never easy being a widow. In the United States today, however, widowhood is not usually as desperate as it was in the Middle East two thousand years ago. In our culture, widows can be wealthy. They can hold positions of influence. And even though many widows face severe financial problems, they are at least allowed to work, attend school and own property.

When Jesus told this story, the situation was quite different. A widow generally had no education, no job, no money, no property, no power, no status. If she had a son, father, or brother-in-law who would care for her, she could survive. If not, she might become a beggar—the first-century equivalent of a street person or a bag lady. She would be a social outcast.

In Jesus' story, the widow had an adversary. Some unnamed local villain was harassing her. Perhaps the person was intimidating her physically; perhaps the person was withholding or stealing funds that should have been used for her support.

In any case, the adversary was winning and she was

losing. The widow had no good way to protect herself, no relatives to see her plight and offer help, no governmental organization to come to her aid. She had only one shot at warding off this villain: she could go before a local judge and plead her case, throwing herself on his mercy. And that is what she decided to do.

The Unjust Judge

Enter the second character: the judge. Jesus described him in two crisp statements: he did not fear God, and he did not respect other human beings.

Without fear of God, this judge had no sense of accountability. He did not respect God's Word, his wisdom or his justice. He did not worry that at some future day of reckoning he would have to give an account for his decisions. Therefore, he made his own justice, decreeing whatever suited his fancy. Like a loaded cannon loosed on deck, he fired wherever he wished.

Without respect for other human beings, this judge did not care how his decisions affected the people who looked for justice in his courtroom. Since people didn't matter to him, he felt free to use and abuse them. He did not see them as brothers and sisters but as problems, interruptions, headaches, hassles. His license plate read *KIKBAK*.

And this judge was the widow's last resort.

It makes you want to say to her, "Don't waste your time going to court. The judge is probably in cahoots with your enemy. He'll laugh in your face and throw you out in the streets." That, of course, is exactly what he did—but the story doesn't end with his dismissal of the case.

Justice Through Pestering

Hurt and shocked by the judge's behavior, the widow gathered her wits and examined her situation one more time. With grim resolve she said to herself, "I don't have any other options. This judge is my only hope. Somehow I must get him to protect me."

But how could she do this? No higher court would hear her case. Penniless, she couldn't even bribe the judge. "I know what I'll do," she said to herself. "I'll pester him. Every time that judge turns around, I'm going to be right in his face. I'll follow him home, I'll follow him to work, I'll follow him to the race track. I'll be on him like a shirt until he offers me protection, puts me in jail or kills me."

So that's what she did—and it worked! She pestered the judge until one day he raised the window in his office and shouted, "I can't take it anymore! Somebody fix this widow's problem. I don't care what it takes. Just do it. She is driving me crazy."

The happy ending to this story is that the crooked, uncaring judge finally gave the widow protection from her adversary. Yet he did not do this from the goodness of his heart but only because of her extraordinary ability to pester him.

A Completely Wrong Interpretation

Luke says Jesus told this story to show his disciples "that they should always pray and not give up" (v. 1). A lot of readers, having come just this far in the story, make a grave error in interpreting it. Thinking of it as an allegory, they look at it like this:

We humans are like the widow. Impoverished, powerless, with no connections and no status, we are unable to handle our problems alone and feel that we have nowhere to turn.

God, then, must be like the judge, these misguided readers continue. He's not really interested in our situation. After all, he has a universe to run, angels to keep in harmony, harps to tune. It's best not to bother him unless it's really important.

If we're desperate, though, we can always do what the widow did: we can pester him. Bang on the doors of heaven. Spend hours on our knees. Ask our friends to pester him too. Sooner or later, we may wear him down and wrench a blessing from his tightly closed fist. Eventually he may shout, "I can't take it anymore—somebody fix this problem!"

Does that interpretation sound right to you? I hope not. But how often I talk with people who seem to think God is like that judge! They are absolutely convinced that the greatest challenge associated with prayer is finding the lost key that will somehow unlock the vault of blessings that God, for some reason, would prefer not to open.

I get tired of reading titles that promise to divulge the secret of getting past God's reluctance, to reveal the little-known way to pester our way into his presence. Please, please don't ever think of God that way! Jesus never meant this story to imply that God is like that callous judge.

Our Responsive God

What, then, does the story mean? Jesus himself interpreted it as soon as he finished telling it. You've heard how the unjust judge reacted, he said; now look at God's approach. "Will not God bring about justice for his chosen ones, who cry out to him day and night? Will he keep putting them off? I tell you, he will see that they get justice, and quickly" (vv. 7-8).

According to Jesus, this story is not an allegory, where elements in the story stand for truths outside the story. Instead it is a parable—a short story with a puzzling aspect that forces listeners to think. This particular parable is a study in opposites. Take a look at the contrasts.

First, we are not like the widow. In fact, we are totally opposite to her. She was poor, powerless, forgotten and abandoned. She had no relationship with the judge. For him, she was just one more item on his to-do list. But we are not abandoned; we are God's adopted sons and daughters, Jesus' brothers and sisters. We are in God's family, and we matter to him. So don't tiptoe into God's presence, trying to find the secret of attracting his attention. Just say, "Hello, Father," and know that he loves to hear your voice.

Second, our loving heavenly Father is nothing like the judge in Jesus' story! The judge was crooked, unrighteous, unfair, disrespectful, uncaring and preoccupied with personal matters. By contrast, our God is righteous and just, holy and tender, responsive and sympathetic.

The psalmist says, "Taste and see that the LORD is good" (Psalm 34:8). Don't think you have to figure out a way to wrench a blessing from him, somehow to trick him into giving up what he would rather keep for himself. God's Word teaches that God loves to bestow blessings on his children. It's his nature; it's who he is—a giving God, a blessing God, an encouraging God, a nurturing God, an empowering God, a loving God.

Abundant Blessings

One of the most theologically enlightening experiences I've ever had occurred when I bought my son a BMX bicycle. He thought *he* was excited—and he was! But after watching him ride it up and down the driveway that first day, I had tears in my eyes when I walked back into the house. I said to my wife, Lynne, "If that bike had cost five hundred dollars, it would have been worth it. I've never gotten more joy from giving a gift to anyone!" I got goosebumps watching him ride that bike, seeing his eyes wide open with excitement. Right then and there I started making plans to buy him a Harley someday—and a car!

Over the years I've heard parents complain, "I have kids that are applying to college and somehow I'll have to cough up the money." Maybe they're kidding when they act so put out. Personally, it has been a great joy to help my kids get a college education. The sacrifices Lynne and I have made do not compare with the growth and development we see in our kids' lives.

I didn't read textbooks to get these feelings. They're just there. I'm just crazy about giving things to my kids. And I'm coming to understand that it gives God great joy to bestow resources and power on his children.

The Bible teaches that we serve a God who is simply looking for opportunities to pour out his blessings on us. It's as if he were saying, "What good are my resources if I don't have anyone to share them with? Just give me a reasonable amount of cooperation, and I will pour out my blessings on you." This theme shows up in the Bible time and time again.

Leviticus 26:3-6 tells us:

If you follow my decrees and are careful to obey my commands, I will send you rain in its season, and the ground will yield its crops and the trees of the field their fruit. Your threshing will continue until grape harvest and the grape harvest will continue until planting, and you will eat all the food you want and live in safety in your land. I will grant peace in the land, and you will lie down and no one will make you afraid. I will remove savage beasts from the land, and the sword will not pass through your country.

Deuteronomy 28:2-6, 12 says:

All these blessings will come upon you and accompany you if you obey the LORD your God: You will be blessed in the city and blessed in the country. The fruit of your womb will be blessed, and the crops of your land and the young of your livestock—the calves of your herds and the lambs of your flocks. Your basket and your kneading trough will be blessed. You will be blessed when you come in and blessed when you go out. The LORD will grant that the enemies who rise up against you will be defeated before you. . . . The LORD will open the heavens, the storehouse of his bounty, to send rain on your land in season and to bless all the work of your hands. You will lend to many nations but will borrow from none.

The words of Nathan the prophet to King David, right after he confessed his adultery with Bathsheba, are especially poignant:

This is what the LORD, the God of Israel, says: "I anointed you king over Israel, and I delivered you from the hand of Saul. . . . I gave you the house of Israel and Judah. And if all this had been too little, I would have given you even more. Why did you despise the word of the LORD by doing what is evil in his eyes?" (2 Samuel 12:7-9)

In other words, "David, I had all kinds of favors and blessings and resources and power that I was going to pour into your life. Why did you mess things up?"

A Rich Inheritance

All through the Old Testament we see the theme that God is ready and willing to share his resources with his people. In the New Testament this concept is extended and made even more precious. There we learn that we have been adopted as God's sons and daughters and have become heirs, along with Jesus Christ, of his glorious kingdom.

Jesus taught us to call God *Father*, actually, *Papa*. The most repeated prayer in the Christian church begins, "Our Father . . ." In love God "predestined us to be adopted as his sons through Jesus Christ" (Ephesians 1:5); "you are no longer a slave but a child, and if a child then also an heir, through God" (Galatians 4:7 NRSV).

In Romans 8:16-17 Paul wrote: "The Spirit himself testifies with our spirit that we are God's children. Now if we are children, then we are heirs—heirs of God and co-heirs with Christ, if indeed we share in his sufferings in order that we may also share in his glory."

What a fantastic promise! God will cover us with blessings because he has adopted us as his sons and daughters! As God's children and legal heirs, we own the world and the universe! Should we ever fear to tell our Father our needs?

Generous Fathers

I had access to anything my father owned, just as soon as I was capable of handling it properly. One of his prized possessions was a forty-five-foot sailboat. When I was in eighth grade, my dad would say to me, "Why don't you get one of your buddies, hitchhike out to South Haven and take the boat out?" Once my brother and I had our driver's licenses, he was equally generous with the car. If he got a new car, the first thing he'd do when he came home was to give us each a set of keys and say, "Take it for a spin. If you want to take it out on a date, go ahead."

Most fathers love to be generous with their children. Jesus understood this, and that is why he used fathers to explain God's generosity:

Which of you, if his son asks for bread, will give him a stone? Or if he asks for a fish, will give him a snake? If you, then, though you are evil, know how to give good gifts to your children, how much more will your Father in heaven give good gifts to those who ask him! (Matthew 7:9-11)

Do you see the picture Jesus is painting? The son has been out in the fields working all day. By the time he comes home, he's famished. The family is at the table, and dishes of steaming, fragrant food are being passed around. Can you imagine a father who would toss the boy a rock and say, "Here, gnaw on this"? Or worse, one who would toss him

an angry snake? No earthly fathers are perfect; we are all
tainted with sin. Even so, we all recognize this as cruel.
Good fathers want to give good gifts to their children—and
so does our heavenly Father.

Our Father's Delight

For some reason, though, most of us have a hard time
accepting the gifts God gives us. In the past when God
would bless me with a special portion of his Spirit, a material
item I had been wanting or a warm new relationship, I can
distinctly remember feeling, *God must have had his wires
crossed. Why would he do that for me?* In fact, I would feel guilty
about my good fortune, as if I had somehow acquired
something that God didn't really want me to have.

I'm learning to give God a little credit. If imperfect fathers
love to bestow blessings on their children, imagine how our
perfect Father in heaven must delight in giving good gifts
to us, his beloved children.

Look again at the statements at the beginning of this
chapter, statements we have all made at one time or another.
Think of how brutal they would sound if they represented
the attitudes of a human father.

☐ I'm busy at the office. I don't want to hear about your
lost bike or unfair teacher.

☐ Don't bother me with your personal needs. I want to take
care of everyone but you. If you really love me, you'll
survive on bread and water.

☐ Sure, I'm rich, but there's no reason I should give you
anything. Back off.

Good fathers don't talk like that. Good fathers are like

my dad. He was a busy man who traveled all over the world. When he was in the office, it was hard to get past the switchboard and several secretaries. That's why he gave a few select business partners, his wife—*and us kids*—his private number. We knew that no matter how busy he was, we could call him anytime and be sure of reaching him.

I also have a private line that rings right on my desk. I've given the number to a few colleagues to use in emergencies, and I've given it to my wife and children. I've told my kids they can call me anytime for any reason. Believe me, no one's voice sounds sweeter to me than theirs. When I hear "Hi Dad," I don't care what I'm juggling. It can drop. My children are an absolute priority to me.

Now take a father's feeling for his children and multiply it exponentially, and you'll know how your heavenly Father feels about you. No one's voice sounds sweeter to God than yours. Nothing in the cosmos would keep him from directing his full attention to your requests.

Is anything holding you back from making them known to him right now?

3

God Is Able

If you could ask God for one miracle in your life, knowing that he would grant your request, would you ask him

☐ to put your marriage back together?

☐ to change something about your job?

☐ to bring home a straying son or daughter?

☐ to heal your body?

☐ to straighten out your finances?

☐ to bring a loved one to Christ?

Whatever your request might be, do you regularly and diligently, every single day, bring to it to God in prayer, trusting that he will intervene in your situation? If not, why not?

Can God Handle It?

Most of us have to admit that we don't pray that often about our deepest needs. We get faint-hearted. We begin to pray, but we soon find our minds wandering, and we realize we're using empty phrases. Our words sound hollow and shallow, and we start to feel hypocritical. Soon we give up. It seems better to live with almost any difficult situation than to continue to pray ineffectively.

We reach out to God, because we know he is holding out loving arms toward us. But then we often fall back and try to face our difficulties in our own power, because at some basic and perhaps unconscious level we doubt if God really can make a difference in the problems we are facing.

It is well and good to believe that God loves us and wants to help us. The question remains: is he *able* to do so? Because if he *isn't*, all the good will in heaven and earth will make no difference.

For years our country has been drowning in a sea of red ink. The federal deficit has dogged us for thirty years. The gap between rich and poor has widened. CEOs pull down princely salaries while mass layoffs multiply, the unskilled cannot find jobs with decent pay, and public aid cannot stem the tide of urban poverty. In spite of the dangerous economic and social situation, however, not one person has ever petitioned me to do something about it—and with good reason. I don't have any power to effect a change in national policy that would solve our economic woes. It would be a waste of your time to ask me to try. That's why nobody ever does, even though the problems are serious and growing.

Parts of our world are perennially torn by war and civil strife—the Middle East, the Balkans, Northern Ireland, parts of Southeast Asia and Africa, Korea. Government corruption, a disregard for human rights and a readiness to use force when words fail all contribute to the loss of much human life every year. Again, no one has ever asked me to do something about these deplorable situations. Why? Because I obviously have no power to bring peace on earth, even though it is desperately needed.

Believing in the Heart

Many of us have pressing personal needs and serious problems that ravage our lives, but we don't ask God for help because somewhere, well beneath our surface layer of faith and trust, we don't believe God has the power to do anything about them.

The fact is, of course, that God is capable of handling any problem we could bring him. Creating planets isn't much of a problem for him. Neither is raising the dead. Nothing is too difficult for God to handle—but he's waiting for us to recognize his power and ask for his help.

I used to make excuses for my faint-hearted prayer life. *I don't have any good models of persevering prayer,* I told myself. *I have too many responsibilities to fulfill, so I don't have the time to pray properly.* But God convinced me that I was not being honest with myself. The real reason my prayers were weak was that my faith was weak.

In my head I have always believed in God's omnipotence. I write about it and preach about it. But too often this belief hasn't registered where it really counts—in my heart. When my heart is not persuaded, I don't pray about difficult situations and ask God to fulfill pressing needs. Somewhere, deep down, I don't believe he can do anything about them.

During my summer study breaks I spend several hours a day reading, planning and praying in a small room over-

looking the harbor in South Haven, Michigan. One morning, watching the waves lapping at the shore, I realized what
the problem in my prayer life was. In my heart I did not
believe that God could do anything about the messes all
around me. Admitting this to God was very embarrassing,
but it was cleansing.

I decided I didn't want to stay where I was, for all
practical purposes disbelieving God's omnipotence. So I
launched an assault on my own lack of conviction. I opened
the Bible and located almost every passage that emphasized
God's ability to accomplish anything he desires.

God's Power over Nature

I looked first at passages that demonstrate God's power over
nature.

When God decided certain seas or rivers needed parting,
he parted them (Exodus 14; Joshua 3). When his people
were hungry, he dropped food from heaven or multiplied
bread and fish (Exodus 16; John 6:1-13). When a storm
endangered the lives of his disciples, he stilled it (Mark
4:35-41). When Israel's troops needed more time to consoli-
date their gains, he extended the daylight hours (Joshua
10:12-14).

One story I especially liked tells about Moses' frustration
when his people were thirsty (Exodus 17:1-7). He brought
their need for water to God, and God said, "See that rock?"

I can imagine Moses saying, "Yes, but what does that
have to do with water? If we need water, let's look at the
ground."

God answered, "No, I don't want you people thinking

you stumbled across an artesian well. I want you to know who has power over nature. I'm going to send you water right out of the side of that dry rock." And he did.

I read and reread all those stories about God's power over nature until once again I was convinced that they really happened in history.

God's Power over Circumstances

Next I looked at God's power to change impossible circumstances.

When the Holy Spirit came to the believers at the first Pentecost, many went out and preached that Christ had come back from the dead and was the Savior of the world. As a result, thousands of people were converted to the new Christian movement. This made both the Roman officials and the traditional Jewish leaders nervous. Threatened by the crowds' enthusiastic response to the Christian preachers, they feared losing their authority over them.

And so the Roman and Jewish leaders resisted the movement. First they arrested several prominent Christians and scolded them publicly. This did no good at all; the Christians said they couldn't help speaking about what they had seen and heard.

Next the officials captured, tortured and imprisoned some of the disciples. This had no lasting effect either. Once released, the disciples spoke with even greater boldness about Christ.

Finally Herod Agrippa, Jerusalem's governor, arrested the apostle James, the brother of John, and had him executed. He then laid plans to put Peter to death also (Acts 12).

Unfortunately for Herod's plans, he had Peter arrested during the Passover feast. Respecting Jewish traditions, he did not want to execute the apostle during Passover week, so Peter was slated to spend several days in jail before losing his head.

To be sure other Christians wouldn't spring their leader, Herod made Peter's security tight. Sixteen Roman soldiers were assigned to guard him. One was chained to his left wrist, one to his right. Sentries guarded the entrance to the cell.

Peter's fellow Christians did not get together to plan a prison break. They knew any human tactics would be futile. Instead they prayed. But Peter remained in jail, and his trial date approached.

Astonished at the Answer

The evening before the scheduled trial and execution, the Christians met at the home of Mary the mother of John Mark to hold an all-night prayer vigil. Peter, confident in Christ whether he lived or died, slept between his captors.

Suddenly an angel of the Lord appeared and a light shone in the cell. He struck Peter on the side and woke him up. "Quick, get up!" he said, and the chains fell off Peter's wrists.

Then the angel said to him, "Put on your clothes and sandals." And Peter did so. "Wrap your cloak around you and follow me," the angel told him. Peter followed him out of the prison, but he had no idea that what the angel was doing was really happening; he thought he was seeing a vision. They passed the first and second guards

and came to the iron gate leading to the city. It opened
for them by itself, and they went through it. When they
had walked the length of one street, suddenly the angel
left him. (Acts 12:7-10)

Baffled, Peter looked around him. Was this real? Was he
free? Had an angel really opened those prison doors? When
the truth dawned on him, he made a beeline for the gathered
believers.

A servant girl answered his knock. Hearing his voice, she
squealed with joy and ran back to tell the praying saints that
their prayers were answered.

"You're out of your mind," they told her. When she kept
insisting that it was so, they said, "It must be his angel."

But Peter kept on knocking, and when they opened
the door and saw him, they were astonished. (vv. 15-16)

The first Christians were no more inclined than contemporary Christians to think that God would miraculously rear-
range circumstances in answer to prayer, but they prayed
anyway. And God rewarded their somewhat incomplete
faith — not by sending them comforting visions but by alter-
ing history.

God's Power over Hearts

Then I looked at passages that reveal God's power to change
people's hearts.

God had the power to make shy Moses a leader (Exodus
3 — 4), to soften cruel Pharaoh's heart (Exodus 11:1-8), to
keep discouraged Elijah from quitting (1 Kings 19:15), to
turn the fanatical persecutor Saul into a globe-trotting
apostle (Acts 9:1-31).

Looking again at the apostle Peter, we see the tremendous difference God's power made in his life. While imprisoned, Peter was so full of faith and peace that he could sleep deeply, even though he thought he would be killed the next day. Ten or fifteen years earlier, Peter had been a different man.

When Jesus was captured in the middle of the night and dragged before religious and civil authorities, most of the disciples ran away in terror. Peter, to his credit, followed his Master right into the high priest's courtyard. But there he lost heart. "They're going to kill him," he thought, "and then they'll start looking for his friends. I'd better put on a pretty good act."

And so Peter, fearing for his life even though no one had threatened it, unsuccessfully tried to change his accent and persuade a group of servants that he had no connections with Jesus.

Jesus knew Peter would deny him, and he also knew that Peter the coward, through God's mighty power, would become Peter the rock, the first major leader of the Christian church (Matthew 16:18-19). "Simon, Simon," Jesus said to Peter the very night of the arrest and denial, "Satan has asked to sift you as wheat. But I have prayed for you, Simon, that your faith may not fail. And when you have turned back, strengthen your brothers" (Luke 22:31-32).

After the crucifixion Peter was a broken man. He couldn't put the pieces back together by himself. Only God's power could change him. And it did, as we see throughout the book of Acts.

As I studied God's power in human lives, once again I

was convinced that God had his way whenever he desired —
in anyone's life he wanted to change. And I reminded myself
that that happened in history, not mythology.

The Same Yesterday, Today and Forever

I studied all these passages because I didn't want simply to
agree with the doctrine of God's omnipotence (I already did
that); I wanted to *own* it, which is a different matter all
together. I wanted to be able to say, "I don't care what other
people think. I don't care about scholars' opinions. I believe
that God has shown his omnipotence in history."

But it's one thing to own the doctrine of God's omnipotence in history; it's quite another to own the doctrine of his
omnipotence today, in my hometown, over my problems
and concerns. To believe this, I must believe that God does
not change, that he is *immutable.*

The doctrine of God's immutability is firmly established
by biblical passages such as Malachi 3:6: "I the LORD do
not change"; or Hebrews 13:8: "Jesus Christ is the same
yesterday and today and forever." God has not changed. He
is not growing old, and his power is not waning. "Do you
not know? Have you not heard? The LORD is the everlast-
ing God, the Creator of the ends of the earth. He will not
grow tired or weary" (Isaiah 40:28). If he ever was able to
control nature, change people and alter circumstances, he
still is able to do these things.

God is able—the Bible repeats the words over and over.
Able to save three of his followers from a fiery furnace
(Daniel 3:17). Able to save Daniel from the lions' mouths
(Daniel 6:20-22). Able to give a child to ninety-year-old

Sarah (Romans 4:18-21). Able to give his followers all that they need (2 Corinthians 9:8). Able to save completely those who come to God through Jesus (Hebrews 7:25). "Able to do immeasurably more than all we ask or imagine" (Ephesians 3:20).

God is able. Just as God has branded that truth into my heart, I have branded those words into a block of wood that I keep where I can see it as I kneel to pray. I value the reminder, because it's an exercise in futility to pray if I don't think God is able to answer.

Whatever it takes for you to own the doctrine of God's omnipotence, do it. Until you own it, you will be a fainthearted pray-er. You'll make a few wishes on your knees, but you won't be able to persevere in prayer until you know in your heart that God is able.

A "prayer warrior" is a person who is convinced that God is omnipotent—that God has the power to do anything, to change anyone and to intervene in any circumstance. A person who truly believes this refuses to doubt God.

Your Personal Invitation

In chapter two we saw that God is eager to pour his good gifts out upon us. Now we know that not only is he willing, he is also able to bless us beyond what we can imagine. But some of us are still hanging back, reluctant to crash uninvited into the presence of the King of the universe.

Hang back no longer! God, through Christ, has issued you a personal invitation to call on him anytime. In fact, it is impossible to come into his presence uninvited, because his Word tells us to "pray continually" (1 Thessalonians 5:17).

If you are not a Christian yet, Jesus' invitation says this: "Come to me, all you who are weary and burdened, and I will give you rest. Take my yoke upon you and learn from me, for I am gentle and humble in heart, and you will find rest for your souls" (Matthew 11:28-29).

If you are already God's child, the invitation is wide open.

You can pray about anything: "Do not be anxious about anything, but in everything, by prayer and petition, with thanksgiving, present your requests to God" (Philippians 4:6).

You don't need to be timid: "Let us then approach the throne of grace with confidence, so that we may receive mercy and find grace to help us in our time of need" (Hebrews 4:16).

Although you pray in Jesus' name, you can be sure that your requests go directly to God: "I am not saying that I will ask the Father on your behalf. No, the Father himself loves you" (John 16:26-27).

It would be foolish not to accept God's invitation: "You do not have, because you do not ask God" (James 4:2).

When you accept God's invitation, miracles begin to happen. You won't believe the changes that will occur in your life — in your marriage, your family, your career, your health, your ministry, your witnessing — once you are convinced in the core of your being that God is willing, that he is able and that he has invited you to come before his throne and do business in prayer.

Waiting for Your Call

God is interested in your prayers because he is interested in you. Whatever matters to you is a priority for his attention. Nothing in the universe matters as much to him as what is going on in your life this day. You don't have to pester him to get his attention. You don't have to spend hours on your knees or flail yourself or go without food to show him you really mean business. He's your Father; he wants to hear what you have to say. In fact, he's waiting for you to call.

If one of my kids ever called me and said, "Dad, please, please, please, I beg you, I petition you, I plead with you to listen to my humble request," I'd say, "Time out. I don't like the underlying assumption here. You don't have to go through all those gymnastics. What in my life is more important than you? What gives me greater pleasure than meeting your needs? What can I do for you?"

"Come into my presence," says God. "Talk to me. Share all your concerns. I'm keenly interested in you, because I'm your Father. I'm able to help, because all power in heaven and earth is mine. And I'm listening very closely, hoping I will hear your voice."

4

Heart-Building Habits

God has invited us to come into his presence. He has told us that he is with us and within us, that he is waiting to hear from us, and that he can and will respond to us. What is more, he has told us what kind of habits we must develop in order to make the most of his blessings.

Some time ago I was helping a friend grieve the sudden loss of his dad. During the course of our conversation he said, "You must have been totally shocked when your dad died at such an early age."

"Well, yes and no," I replied. "The morning my brother called and told me he had just died of a heart attack — that was a shock. But that he would die young was not a shock at all."

My father's death was predictable because he had a horrendous family history of heart disease. Even more important, he had terrible health habits. He used to say, "I don't eat anything that hasn't been cooked in thirty-weight

Havoline motor oil." He did not exercise. He did not have regular hours for sleep. And he was in a fast-paced, high-stress job his entire adult life.

Because of the lifestyle he chose, he suffered from indigestion, heartburn and high blood pressure. He carried twenty extra pounds, could not walk at a fast pace and experienced serious dips in energy. Near the end of his life he couldn't even do the basic sail-handling chores on his beloved boat. His bad habits not only led to an early death; they also made his life uncomfortable.

The Quest for the Magic Wand

Our spirits, like our bodies, have requirements for health and growth. Some people don't want to pay the price of developing good spiritual habits. Sadly, they end up paying the much higher price of spiritual disease and even death.

Last year a man came to me in despair. "I lost my job," he told me. "I've spent months looking for another position, to no avail." And unemployment was not his worst problem. He went on: "I feel so alone in this. Nobody in the church cares. Sometimes I think God doesn't care. I feel totally hopeless and helpless."

I asked the man about his spiritual habits. Was he taking responsibility for feeding his faith? How often did he pray—commune with God and listen for his prompting? Did he regularly attend church services? Was he maintaining friendships with any spiritually minded people? Was he reaching out to help meet others' needs?

No, the man said, he was doing none of these things. "I just can't find the time," he explained. I subtly reminded him that, being unemployed and single, he was probably richer in time than in any other resource. He gave me a look I've seen before, one that seemed to say, "Hey, I have problems. The last thing I need when I'm down on my luck is a list of to-dos from a pastor."

That man wanted someone to wave a magic wand and offer him courage. He said he wanted God's presence in his life, but he did not want to form any habits that would increase his spiritual health.

Straitjacket Discipline

When we make a habit of prayer, we stay constantly tuned to God's presence and open to receive his blessings. How do we make prayer a habit? Jesus laid out some principles. But before we discuss them, I must issue two warnings.

The first warning is for those who love lists and formulas. You take notes during talks and underline when you read, and you already practice a rigorous spiritual regimen. Before you dutifully lengthen your list of spiritual duties, back off. Do you need more habits—or more effective ones? Do you need to weigh yourself down further—or bring your heavy load to Jesus?

I fear that for too many believers, spiritual discipline turns into a straitjacket experience filled with requirements that squeeze the vitality and spontaneity and adventure right out of faith and life. For these people, Christ no longer brings freedom. Religion becomes a heavy burden. Most people can't live that way for long. Some of those who really work at it develop such a self-righteous attitude that everyone wishes they would fail.

Galatians 5:1 warns the list-lovers: "It is for freedom that Christ has set us free. Stand firm, then, and do not let yourselves be burdened again by a yoke of slavery."

A Nonnegotiable Decision

My second warning is for those who make the equal and opposite error. You are thinking, *I don't need any structure or rigorous habits to make my heart grow. I'm a play-it-by-ear type. I go with the spiritual flow. I'm going to let go and let God do whatever he wants to do, and I'll just see what happens.*

This typical American attitude, at best, is naive; at worst, it is self-deceived. We just cannot grow with no structure, no sense of intentionality about our spiritual life, any more than we can lower our body fat or develop good muscle tone or increase our net worth by just sitting back and waiting for whatever happens.

If a goal is really important to me, I discipline myself in order to achieve it. I decide *in advance* that practicing to meet the goal is nonnegotiable. Otherwise—count on it—I bail out at the last moment. For example, one of my big goals is to stay alive and healthy. I know that with my genetic endowment, I would be crazy not to exercise faithfully every day. So I have made a decision: I will jog, and my jogging time is nonnegotiable.

I don't wait to jog until I feel like running. Let's be honest—how many days a week do I really want to do it? Not today—I need to stay at work longer. My biorhythms aren't right. It's a little chilly outside. It's going to rain. It's too sunny. My shoes are tight. My knees ache. My couch looks inviting. The list is endless.

When we get serious about learning to pray, it's time to make a decision: *I will learn what disciplines are necessary to my prayer life, and I will practice these disciplines regularly, without fail.*

Maintaining good prayer habits is nonnegotiable. I know that no discipline will, in and of itself, create a relationship between God and me. At the same time, I know that I will not develop a rich, rewarding prayer life if I try to do it without discipline.

Ask an Expert

So how can we learn the heart-building habits of prayer, the practices that expand our freedom and give us spiritual wings? According to a well-known business axiom, "If you want to know something, ask an expert." If you want to know about basketball, ask Michael Jordan. If you want to learn how to conduct an interview, ask Katie Couric. If you want to understand the computer business, ask Bill Gates.

It makes sense, then, if you want to learn good prayer habits, to ask the number-one expert—Jesus Christ himself.

No one in history has ever understood prayer better than Jesus. No one has ever believed more strongly in the power of prayer, and no one has ever prayed as he did. His disciples recognized his expertise. Once they stumbled upon him while he was praying privately (see Luke 11:1). They were so moved by his earnestness and intensity that when he finally got up from his knees, one of them timidly asked, "Would you teach us to pray?" They knew that in comparison to their Master, they were mere neophytes—first-graders in the school of prayer.

Jesus' Prayer Principles

Jesus did not object to their question. Instead, he took the opportunity to teach them how to pray. This is what he said:

> When you pray, do not be like the hypocrites, for they love to pray standing in the synagogues and on the street corners to be seen by men. . . . When you pray, go into your room, close the door and pray to your Father, who is unseen. Then your Father, who sees what is done in secret, will reward you. And when you pray, do not keep on babbling like pagans, for they think they will be heard because of their many words. Do not be like them, for your Father knows what you need before you ask him.
>
> This, then, is how you should pray: "Our Father in heaven, hallowed be your name, your kingdom come, your will be done on earth as it is in heaven. Give us today our daily bread. Forgive us our debts, as we also have forgiven our debtors. And lead us not into temptation, but deliver us from the evil one." (Matthew 6:5-13)

No other passage in Scripture tells so straightforwardly how to pray, and the advice Jesus offered his disciples two thousand years ago applies to all of us today:

☐ *Pray regularly.* Jesus said, *"When* you pray," not *"if* you pray."

☐ *Pray privately.* God is not impressed by public displays of piety.

☐ *Pray sincerely.* God is not interested in formulas. He wants to hear what is on our hearts.

☐ *Pray specifically.* Take the prayer we call the Lord's Prayer or the "Our Father" as a model.

In the next chapter, we will look at Jesus' prayer principles one at a time. We will also look at some heart-building habits—disciplines, practices, methods—that can help us incorporate these principles into our prayer lives.

5

Praying Like Jesus

When the disciples asked Jesus for instruction on prayer, Jesus began by saying, "When you pray..." (Matthew 6:5). He simply assumed the disciples would have a regular time for prayer.

That's a big assumption to make about Jesus' disciples today. Most of us say we just don't have time for daily prayer. But do we want prayer to become a vital part of our lives? If we want to develop in any other area—piano, basketball, physical fitness—we practice regularly. The America's Cup team from New Zealand practiced intensively for two years, six days a week, eight hours a day, and they brought sailing maneuvers to a level never before achieved. People who are serious about something always make room for it in their schedules.

It is important to have a regular time for prayer, because without regularity prayer will never become a habit. If we want to live in God's presence, we need to shut the world out and tune in to God once a day, every day, without fail. We need to lay aside our other concerns and focus on God, look at him, talk with him, listen to him, sit quietly before him.

Get Away from Distractions

If establishing a regular prayer time is important, so is making a regular prayer place. Some people pray in public places, at social gatherings and at mealtimes, just so they can be seen and heard and assumed to be religious. But prayer, Jesus says, is not a spectator sport. It is not something we are to engage in to give off signals of spirituality. Forget that idea, says Jesus. When you pray, go into your room and shut the door. Find a closet, an empty office, the workshop out in the garage, some secret place away from people and alone with God. That's where you can pray most effectively.

Why the emphasis on privacy? Why shut the door? First, there is an obvious, practical reason. A private place ensures a minimum of distractions, and most people find distractions deadly when it comes to making connection with God. Almost any kind of noise—voices, music, a ringing phone, kids, dogs, birds—can cause me to lose my concentration during a time of prayer. Even a ticking clock can catch me up in its rhythm until I'm tapping my foot and singing a country song to its beat. Jesus knows how our minds are put together, and he counsels, "Don't bother fighting distractions, because you'll lose. Avoid them. Find a quiet place where you can pray without interruption."

The practical reasons for privacy are important, but I

think there is also a more subtle wisdom in Jesus' advice to pray in a secret place. Once you identify such a place and begin to use it regularly, a kind of aura surrounds it. Your prayer room, even if it is a laundry room in the basement, becomes to you what the Garden of Gethsemane became to Jesus—a holy place, the place where God meets with you.

Create a Special Atmosphere

Some married couples have a favorite restaurant where they go for important nights out. They love the atmosphere. They find it easy to talk in that environment, and they look forward to going there. It's a special place in their relationship.

Some families have a regular vacation spot that feels almost like a second home to them. Great things happen to the family there; special memories are created. The families look forward to their vacation times.

In a similar way, when you create a secret place where you can really pray, over time you will look forward to going there. You will begin to appreciate the familiar surroundings, sights and smells. You will grow to love the aura of the place where you freely converse with God.

I created such a prayer room near the credenza in a corner of my former office. In my prayer place I put an open Bible, a sign that says "God is able," a crown of thorns to remind me of the suffering Savior, and a shepherd's staff that I often hold up while making requests.

That office corner became a holy place for me. I arrived there around six o'clock in the morning, when no one was around and the phone was unlikely to ring, and there I communed with the Lord. I poured out my heart to him, worshiped him, prayed for members of my congregation and received remarkable answers to prayer.

My office has since been relocated, and I now have a new prayer corner. But I have warm memories of the old one — not because there is anything holy about the corner itself but because of what happened there. Every morning for several years I met with the Lord, and he faithfully met with me. Thinking of that corner is like thinking of home.

If you want to learn how to pray, find yourself a quiet place free of distractions. It doesn't have to be a chapel. It can be the utility room, the kitchen pantry, the barn, your office or the front seat of your pickup truck, as long as the surroundings are familiar and quiet. Go there during the best part of your day — in the morning if you're a lark, late at night if you're an owl or whatever time you feel most alert. Meet with the Lord there regularly, every day.

Mean What We Say

Not only did Jesus tell his disciples to pray secretly; he also told them to pray sincerely. "Do not keep on babbling," he said. Be careful of clichés. Don't fall into the habit of using meaningless repetition.

How easy it is to use sanctified jargon while praying! Certain phrases sound so appropriate, so spiritual, so pious, that many people learn to string them together and call that prayer. They may not even think of the implications of what they are saying.

For example, I sometimes hear a mature Christian say very earnestly, "Dear Lord, please be with me as I go on this new job interview," or "Please be with me as I go on this trip." When you first hear it, this request sounds holy. Unfortunately, it doesn't make sense. I'm often tempted to ask the one who is praying, "Why do you ask God to do what he is already doing?"

In Matthew 28:20 Jesus says, "Surely I am with you always, to the very end of the age." In Hebrews 13:5 God says, "Never will I leave you; never will I forsake you." Jesus tells his disciples in John 14:18, "I will not leave you as orphans; I will come to you." One of Jesus' names, Emmanuel, means "God with us." We don't need to ask God to be with us if we are members of his family. Instead, we need to pray that we will be *aware* of his presence, that we will be confident because of it. Asking God to be with us when he is already there is one kind of "babbling."

Another kind of meaningless repetition is often heard at the dinner table. A person sits down to a meal that is a nutritional nightmare. The grease is bubbling, the salt is glistening, the sugared drink stands ready to slosh the stuff down. "Dear Lord," the person prays, "bless this food to our bodies, and grant us strength and nourishment from it so that we may do your will." God's will might be for the person to say "Amen," push back from the table and give the meal to the dog—except that dogs matter to God too!

The apostle Paul tells us God's will in 1 Corinthians 6:20: "Honor God with your body." That means putting the right things into your body. Don't ask God to bless junk food and miraculously transform it so that it has nutritional value. Doing that is acting like the fifth-grader who, after taking the geography test, prayed, "Dear God, please make Detroit the capital of Michigan." That's not how God works.

Pray from the Heart

God doesn't want us to pile up impressive phrases. He doesn't want us to use words without thinking about their meaning. He wants us simply to talk to him as to a friend or father—authentically, reverently, personally, earnestly. I heard a man do this once when I least expected it.

I attended a conference at which a number of high-level Christian leaders were present. The conversation was intense; I had to strain to keep up with the theological and philosophical issues being discussed. Lunchtime came, and we all gathered at a nearby restaurant, the Hole in the Wall. A seminary professor was asked to pray. As we bowed our heads I thought, *This prayer is going to sound like theology class.*

The theologian began to pray. "Father," he said, "I love being alive today. And I love sitting down with brothers in the Hole in the Wall, eating good food and talking about kingdom business. I know you're at this table, and I'm glad. I want to tell you in front of these brothers that I love you, and I'll do anything for you that you ask me to do."

He went on talking like that for another minute or two. When he said "Amen," I thought, *I have some growing to do.* His sincere prayer showed me how often I pray on automatic pilot. But God isn't interested in stock phrases. Psalm 62:8 says, "Pour out your hearts to him." Talk to him. Say, "Lord, this is how I feel today. I've been thinking about this recently. I'm worried about this. I'm depressed about that. I'm happy about this." Talk to the Father sincerely.

Pray Specifically

Besides praying privately and sincerely, Jesus counseled his disciples to pray specifically. He showed them what he meant by giving them a model prayer, the prayer we have come to call the Lord's Prayer.

Jesus' prayer begins with the words *Our Father.* Never forget that if you are God's child through Jesus Christ, you are praying to a Father who couldn't love you more than he already does.

The next phrase, *who art in heaven,* is a reminder that God is sovereign, majestic and omnipotent. Nothing is too difficult for him. He is the mountain mover; he is bigger than any problem you could bring to him. Fix your eyes on his ability, not on your worth.

Hallowed be thy name. Don't let your prayers turn into a wish list for Santa Claus. Worship God and praise him when you come to him in prayer.

Thy kingdom come, thy will be done, on earth as it is in heaven. Submit your will to God's. Put his will first in your life — in your marriage, family, career, ministry, money, body, relationships, church.

Give us this day our daily bread. The apostle Paul wrote, "In everything, by prayer and petition, with thanksgiving, present your requests to God" (Philippians 4:6). Lay out all your concerns, whether big or small. If you need a miracle, ask for it without shrinking back.

Forgive us our debts, as we forgive our debtors. Be sure you're not the obstacle: confess your sins, receive forgiveness and begin to grow. Live with a forgiving spirit toward others.

Lead us not into temptation, but deliver us from evil. Pray for protection from evil and victory over temptation.

For thine is the kingdom, and the power, and the glory forever. End your prayer with more worship. Acknowledge that everything in heaven and earth is God's. Thank the Lord for caring about you, for making it possible for you to talk to him through prayer.

Amen. Let it be so.

God-honoring prayers are not simply shopping lists. They are more than cries for help, strength, mercy and miracles. Authentic prayer should include worship: "Our Father in heaven, hallowed be your name" (Matthew 6:9). It should include submission: "Your will be done on earth as it is in heaven" (v. 10). Requests are certainly appropriate: "Give us today our daily bread" (v. 11); as are confessions: "Forgive us our debts, as we also have forgiven our debtors" (v. 12).

The Lord's Prayer is an excellent model, but it was never intended to be a magical incantation to get God's attention. Jesus didn't give this prayer as a paragraph to be recited; in fact, he had just warned against using repetitious phrases. Instead, he gave it as a pattern to suggest the variety of elements that should be included when we pray.

Reflect on Your Time with God

The trouble with magical incantations is that they are mindless. Too often we go through life without thinking about what we're doing and what it all means. If we approach prayer thoughtlessly, we can't expect powerful results.

I used to be the chaplain for the Chicago Bears. Every Monday during the season I would lead a Bible study in

Halas Hall. Often I'd get there a little early and listen in as the coaches worked with the team. I was struck by how Mike Ditka and the other coaches would replay each individual play of the previous day's game. Before moving into preparations for the next game, the team would reflect on the one they had just played.

At that same time I was reading Christian authors who were saying that if Christ's followers don't grow, it's because they do not make a habit of evaluating their lives. Those authors were describing me. I was moving fast, always on the go but never looking deeply inside. I never did the kind of reflection that leads to growth. And I was paying the price—committing the same stupid sins over and over, living with the same heavy load of guilt.

So I made a difficult decision. I decided that each day I would try to honestly assess my soul's condition. I would look inside myself, and I would write down what I saw. Feeling awkward and embarrassed, I took out a spiral notebook and started to write. "God, here are some frustrations in my life. They aren't going away, so I might as well take a look at them." Or, "Here's a relationship I'm concerned about. It's not good, and I don't know how to improve it." Or, "Here are some blessings you've poured into my life." After writing a paragraph or two, I would reflect on what I had written.

Above All, Pray!

It's been nearly fifteen years since I started writing reflections about my day. I soon began writing out my whole prayer and reading it back to God. I've been blessed in many ways because of this discipline. It helps me concentrate. I used to get no further than "Dear God" and I'd already be thinking of the person I was going to meet for lunch, or the board meeting agenda, or what my family would be doing after dinner. When I'm moving a pen across paper, it is much easier to keep focused. Writing also forces me to be specific; broad generalities don't look good on paper. And it helps me see when God answers prayers.

At the end of each month, I read over my prayer journal and see where God has done miraculous things. Whenever my faith feels weak, I turn to my journal and see evidence that God is answering my prayers. If I can list a number of answers to specific prayers in January, I feel better prepared to trust God in February.

I write out my prayers every day; I have not been able to grow in my prayer life any other way. Experiment and see what works best for you. Try writing out your prayers once a week at first. If you find it helpful, do it more often. If it cramps your style and makes you uncomfortable, find another way that is more effective for you.

Whatever helpful disciplines you choose, practice praying Jesus' way. Make your prayers regular, private, sincere and specific.

Remember that God's prevailing power is released through prayer. He is interested in you and your needs. He is able to meet any need, and he has invited you to pray. His Son, Jesus, the expert on prayer, has given instructions so that you know just how to pray.

For the miracle of prayer to begin operating in our lives, we must finally do only one thing: we must pray. I can write about prayer, and you can read about it, and you can even lend my book to a friend. But sooner or later, we have to pray. Then, and only then, will we begin to live moment by moment in God's presence.

6

A Pattern for Prayer

You've decided it's high time to get into good physical
shape, so you investigate a health club. When you walk in
the door, you are greeted by a staff member who takes you
from station to station, showing you the state-of-the-art
equipment. At the end of the orientation your guide asks,
"Would you like us to set up a routine for you?"

At this point you may feel like backing out. Playing on
exercise equipment is one thing; following an established
regimen is quite another. Seeing your hesitation, the staff
member explains: "You need a routine in order to work all
the muscle groups properly and consistently, to keep track
of how many repetitions you've done at which weight, to
chart your progress and to avoid becoming imbalanced."

Looking around the fitness center, you see examples of
serious imbalance. A behemoth with bulging deltoids walks
out of the weight room. Still wearing his weight belt, he
stumbles and gasps a couple of times around the track

before gratefully returning to familiar territory. Then you see a guy glide effortlessly around the track. He probably does seven miles at a time, but from his upper-body appearance, you know his wife has to open the pickle jars and carry in the logs to stock the fireplace.

Health-club instructors know that without a carefully structured plan, we're all likely to become imbalanced. That's because we all tend to do what we enjoy and ignore the difficult or distasteful or untried.

A Pattern for Prayer

Developing prayer fitness is like developing physical fitness: we need a pattern to avoid becoming imbalanced. Without a routine, we will probably fall into the "Please God" trap: "Please God, give me. Please God, help me. Please God, cover me. Please God, arrange this."

Oh, occasionally we'll toss a few thanks heavenward when we notice that God has allowed some good thing to come our way. Every once in a while, if we get caught with our hand in the cookie jar, we'll confess a momentary lapse of sound judgment. And now and then, if we're feeling really spiritual, we might even throw a little worship into our prayers—but only as the Spirit leads.

If I sound sarcastic, it's because I know all about imbalanced prayer—I'm a real pro in that department. And I can tell you from personal experience where imbalanced prayer leads. Sensing the carelessness and one-sidedness of our prayers, we begin to feel guilty about praying. Guilt leads to faint-heartedness, and that in turn leads to prayerlessness. When praying makes us feel guilty, pretty soon we stop praying.

If that has happened to you, it's time to set up a prayer routine.

I'm going to offer you a pattern to follow. It's not the only pattern or the perfect pattern, but it's a good pattern that has been used for many years in Christian circles. It's balanced, and it's easy to use. All you have to remember is the word *ACTS*, an acrostic whose four letters stand for *adoration, confession, thanksgiving* and *supplication.*

Adoration: Entering Holy Space

In my opinion, it is absolutely essential to begin times of prayer with adoration, or worship.

Adoration sets the tone for the entire prayer. It reminds us whom we are addressing, whose presence we have entered, whose attention we have gained. How often our problems and trials and needs seem so pressing that we reduce prayer to a wish list! But when we commit ourselves to beginning all our prayers with adoration, we have to slow down and focus our attention on God.

Walking into some churches, we are gripped for a moment. We say to ourselves, "This is holy ground. I need to concentrate, to focus on what's going on here." Our initial pause adds meaning to the service that follows. Likewise, when we begin our prayers with adoration, we set the tone for our meeting with God.

Adoration reminds us of God's identity and inclination. As we list his attributes, lifting up his character and personality, we reinforce our understanding of who he is.

Often I begin my prayers by saying, "I worship you for your omnipotence." When I say that, I'm reminded that

God is able to help me, no matter how difficult my problem seems to me.

I also worship him for his omniscience. No mystery confounds God; he will not have to scratch his head about anything I say.

I worship God for his omnipresence. Wherever I'm praying—in an airplane, in my car or on some remote island—I know he is present with me.

We can praise God for being faithful, righteous, just, merciful, gracious, willing to provide, attentive, unchanging. When in a spirit of adoration we begin going through God's attributes, we soon say from the heart, *I am praying to a tremendous God!* And that motivates us to continue praying.

Adoration purifies the one who is praying. When we have spent a few minutes praising God for who he is, our spirit is softened and our agenda changes. Those burning issues we were dying to bring to God's attention may seem less crucial. Our sense of desperation subsides as we focus on God's greatness, and we can truly say, "I am enjoying you, God; it is well with my soul." Adoration purges our spirit and prepares us to listen to God.

God is worthy of adoration. It should be hard to get past the "Our Father" in our prayer without falling back in awe at that incredible miracle. "How great is the love the Father has lavished on us, that we should be called children of God!" (1 John 3:1). A God who is omnipotent, omniscient and omnipresent and yet who loves us, watches over us, gives us good gifts—this is amazing! Our heavenly Father is worthy of our worship, and so right at the beginning let's offer it to him.

How to Adore God

How do we adore God? What better way than to list his attributes? Sometimes I think of every attribute I can. Other times I focus on one I have been especially aware of in recent days. When facing major decisions, I may concentrate on his guidance. When suffering from a feeling of inadequacy or guilt, I may praise him for his mercy. When in need, I may worship him for his providence or power.

Pick out a psalm of praise and read or say it to him. Some of the best known are Psalms 8, 19, 23, 46, 95, 100 and 148; but go through the whole book and see what you can find. Two other wonderful psalms of praise are the Magnificat (Luke 1:46-55) and Zechariah's song (Luke 1:68-79). And if you're in a closed room that's soundproof, why not sing God a song?

Adoration is foreign to most Americans, and you will probably feel clumsy when you first do it. As with anything else you take up—racquetball, computer programming or a new job—you have to get disciplined, stretch yourself and work at it to do it well. After a while you progress in both comfort and proficiency. Adoration becomes a necessity in your prayer life. You can no longer get along without it.

Confession: Naming Our Faults

Confession is probably the most neglected area in personal prayer today. We often hear people pray publicly, "Lord, forgive us for our many sins." A lot of us carry that approach into our private prayer. We throw all our sins onto a pile without so much as looking at them, and we say, "God, please cover the whole dirty heap."

This approach to confession, unfortunately, is a colossal cop-out. When I lump all my sins together and confess them en masse, it's not too painful or embarrassing. But if I take those sins out of the pile one by one and call them by name, it's a whole new ball game.

I determined that in my prayers, I would deal with sin specifically. I would say, "I told so-and-so there were nine hundred cars in the parking lot when really there were only six hundred. That was a lie, and therefore I am a liar. I plead for your forgiveness for being a liar."

Or instead of admitting I had been less than the best husband, I would say, "Today I willfully determined to be self-centered, uncaring and insensitive. It was a calculated decision. I walked through the door thinking, *I'm not going to serve her tonight. I had a hard day, and I deserve to have things my way.* I need your forgiveness for the sin of selfishness."

Who's a Sinner?

Many years ago I had an interesting conversation with a man — I'll call him Harry — who regularly attended my church. I had given a message on our sinfulness and our need for a Savior. Harry came to my office and said, "All this talk about sin is making me feel really bad. I for one don't consider myself a sinner."

Harry was a guy I could shoot straight with, and so I said, "Well, maybe you're not. Let me ask you a few questions. You've been married twenty-five years. Have you been absolutely one hundred percent faithful to your wife the whole time?"

He chuckled and said, "Well, you know, I'm in sales. I

travel a lot . . ." We both knew what he was admitting to.

"Okay," I said, "when you fill out your expense account, do you ever add something that wasn't strictly business?"

"Everybody does that," he replied.

"And when you are out there selling your product, do you ever exaggerate — say it will do something it won't, or promise to ship it tomorrow when you know it won't go out until next Tuesday?"

"That's the industry standard," he said.

I looked straight at him and said, "You have just told me that you are an adulterer, a cheater and a liar. Repeat those words after me — *I am an adulterer, a cheater and a liar.*"

He looked as if his eyes were going to pop out. "Don't use those awful words!" he said. "I only said there was a little something on the side, a little this and a little that . . ."

"No," I said. "Just say it like it is. You're an adulterer, a cheater and a liar. To me, that means you're a sinner in desperate need of a Savior."

The Benefits of Confession

I don't know what happened to Harry. After that encounter, I didn't see a lot of him. I'm hoping that someday he will own up to his sinfulness and find cleansing in Jesus Christ. But I know what will happen to *you* when you have the courage to call your sins by their true names.

First, your conscience will be cleansed. *I finally said it,* you will think. *I'm finally getting honest with God. I'm not playing games anymore, and it feels good.*

Next, you will be flooded with relief that God has a forgiving nature. Knowing that "as far as the east is from the west, so far has he removed our transgressions from us" (Psalm 103:12), you will begin to learn the meaning of peace.

Then you will feel free to pray, "Please give me your strength to forsake that sin from here on out." With the power of the Holy Spirit, you can make a commitment to give up the sin and to live for Christ. And that's when your life begins to show signs of change.

I don't think many of us Christians take confession seriously enough. If we did, our lives would be radically different. When you're totally honest about your sins, something happens. About the fifth day in a row that you have to call yourself a liar, a greedy person, a manipulator or whatever, you say to yourself, *I'm tired of admitting that. With God's power, I've got to root it out of my life.*

As God goes to work on your sins, you begin to see Paul's words being fulfilled in your life: "If anyone is in Christ, he is a new creation; the old has gone, the new has come!" (2 Corinthians 5:17).

Thanksgiving: Expressing Gratitude

The *T* in *ACTS* stands for *thanksgiving.* Psalm 103:2 says, "Praise the Lord, O my soul, and forget not all his benefits." Paul writes in 1 Thessalonians 5:18, "Give thanks in all circumstances, for this is God's will for you in Christ Jesus."

Some of us have not made a simple distinction. There is a difference between feeling grateful and expressing thanks. The classic teaching on this is in Luke 17:11-19, the story of the ten men healed of leprosy. How many of those men do you think felt tremendous gratitude as they walked away from Jesus, completely healed of their incurable, disgusting, socially isolating disease? There's no question about it—all ten did. But how many came back, threw themselves at Jesus' feet and thanked him? Just one.

In this story we catch a glimpse of Jesus' emotions. He is moved: first to disappointment by people who felt gratitude but didn't take the time to express it, then to satisfaction by the one who came all the way back to say thanks.

Parents, you know how it feels when one of your children spontaneously thanks you for something. One summer I took my son Todd to the county fair. We enjoyed some rides, and my tired little boy fell asleep in the back seat as we started home. A few minutes down the highway, though, he had his arms around my shoulders. "Dad, I want to thank you for taking me to that fair," he said. His words moved me so much, I felt like turning the car around and going back for round two! God is our Father, and he too is moved when we express our thanksgiving.

I thank God every day for four kinds of blessings: answered prayers, spiritual blessings, relational blessings and material blessings. Almost everything in my life fits into one of those categories. By the time I've gone through each category, I'm ready to go back to adoration for all God has done for me.

Supplication: Asking for Help

But then it's time for *supplications*—requests. Philippians 4:6 says, "In everything, by prayer and petition, with thanksgiving, present your requests to God." If you have adored him, confessed your sins and thanked him for all his good gifts, you're ready to tell him what you need.

Nothing is too big for God to handle or too small for him to be interested in. Still, I sometimes wonder if my requests are legitimate. So I'm honest with God. I say, "Lord, I don't know if I have the right to ask for this. I don't know how I should pray about it. But I lift it to you, and if you'll tell me how to pray, I'll pray your way."

God honors that kind of prayer. James says, "If any of you lacks wisdom, he should ask God, who gives generously to all without finding fault, and it will be given to him" (James 1:5).

Other times, when I think I know how to pray, I say, "God, this is my heart on the matter, and I'd really like you to do this. But if you have other plans, far be it from me to get in the way. You've asked me to make my requests known, and that's what I'm doing. But if what I'm asking for isn't a good gift, if the time isn't right, if I'm not ready to receive it, no problem. Your ways are higher than my ways, and your thoughts than my thoughts. If you have different plans, we'll go your way."

I break my requests down into categories: ministry, people, family and personal.

Under *ministry,* I pray for the church staff, the construction programs, the public services and all the subministries of our church. I pray that through our ministry God will draw people to himself by confronting them with the living Christ and rescuing them from emptiness, alienation and hell.

Under *people,* I pray for Christian brothers and sisters in leadership positions, the elders, the board, the sick. I pray for the people far from God in my circle of friends, that God will draw them to himself.

Under *family*, I pray for my marriage and for my children. I ask God to make me a godly husband. I ask him for help with decisions about finances, education, vacation time.

Under *personal*, I pray about my character. I say, "God, I want to be more righteous. Whatever you have to bring into my life to transform my character, bring it on. I want to be conformed to the image of Christ."

Break up your requests into whatever categories suit your purposes, and then keep a list of what you've prayed about. After about three weeks, go back and reread your list. Find out what God has already done. In many cases, you will be amazed.

ACTS and Written Prayers

I've found the ACTS formula especially helpful when I write out my prayers. Starting with *adoration*, I might write something like this: "Good morning, Lord! I feel free to praise you today, and I'm choosing this moment when I'm fresh and ready, willing and able to get going, to stop and say that I love you. You are a wonderful God. Your personality and character bring me to my knees. You are holy, just, righteous, gracious, merciful, fair, tender, loving, fatherly and forgiving. I'm thrilled to be in a relationship with you today, and I worship you now."

After adoration I move to *confession*. I might write: "Please forgive me for committing the sin of partiality. It is so much easier for me to direct my love and attention toward those who seem to 'have it all together.' Without even realizing it, I find myself avoiding troubled people. I'm sorry. Thanks for your impartiality to me. Please forgive me, and now I claim your forgiveness." Then I take my pen and cross out what I've written, saying, "I thank you that I'm free from this. I'm glad the slate is clean. Thank you for forgiving me."

Thanksgiving is easy for me. I thank God for specific answers to prayer, for helping me in my work, for people's responsiveness, for protecting our elders, staff and board, for material and relational blessings and for anything else that makes me particularly happy. Thanking the Lord every day keeps me from being covetous, and putting my thanks on paper reminds me of the incredible number of blessings I enjoy.

I'm glad that *supplication* is last. Once I've worshiped God, confessed my sins, and given thanks, it's okay for me to take out my shopping list. In fact, James 4:2 says, "You do not have, because you do not ask God." I used to be vague about what I needed. "Please help me and cover me and keep me out of trouble." I don't do that anymore. I list specific requests, leave them with God and regularly review them to see how he has answered them.

When I get up from praying, I feel as if a ton of bricks has been lifted off my shoulders. 1 Peter 5:7 says, "Cast all your anxiety on him because he cares for you." When I pray, I'm not just telling God my problems. I'm turning my biggest concerns over to him. Once I've put them in his capable hands, I can go about my day in his strength, free from crushing concerns.

Getting Started

Here are two assignments to get your prayer routine

started. Try one today and one tomorrow and see which works better for you.

Write it down. Take a sheet of paper and draw three horizontal lines across it, dividing it into four sections. Label the sections *A, C, T* and *S.*

In the first section, write a paragraph of adoration. List God's characteristics that especially move you today.

In the second, write a paragraph of confession. Specifically identify the sins that are on your conscience. (You can burn this paper when you're done with it!)

In the third, list God's blessings for which you are thankful.

And in the fourth, make your requests, whatever they may be.

Say it out loud. Turn to page 189, "A Guide for Private or Group Prayer." Follow the prayer suggestions, reading the Scripture verses aloud and adding your own prayers as prompted. You can use this for your private devotions or for group prayer. You may decide to write out your personal prayers but use the liturgy when you are praying with others.

Keep it up. Pray one way or the other today, and again tomorrow and the next day. Experiment with the ACTS routine. Adapt the categories to fit your situation, but be sure to include each category each time you pray. Experience the blessings of balance.

And see what God does in your life.

7

Mountain-Moving Prayer

Jesus said, "I tell you the truth, if you have faith and do not doubt, . . . you can say to this mountain, 'Go, throw yourself into the sea,' and it will be done. If you believe, you will receive whatever you ask for in prayer" (Matthew 21:21-22).

According to the Bible, believers can be confident that their prayers will be answered. Our prayers are more than wishes, hopes or feeble aspirations—but only if we pray with believing, faith-filled hearts. That is the kind of prayer that moves mountains.

Jesus, of course, was not in the excavation business. He had little interest in relocating piles of rocks in the ocean's depths. He was using the term *mountain* figuratively. Whatever mountain stands in your path, whatever obstacle blocks your way, whatever difficulty immobilizes you, the prayer of faith can remove it.

That sounds good, but how can we learn to pray with a

faith-filled heart? How can we develop the confidence that removes roadblocks?

I could list some generic guidelines for building a faith that moves mountains, but I honestly don't think that reading lists is the best way to strengthen confidence in God. So I'm going to try a different approach. First, I'll give just two practical principles. Then I'll show them in action, one in my lifetime and one three thousand years ago.

Don't Focus on the Mountain

The first principle is this: *Faith comes from looking at God, not at the mountain.*

Some years ago, a member of my church's vocal team and I were invited by a Christian leader to go to southern India. There we would join a ministry team of people from various parts of the United States. We were told that God would use us to reach Muslims and Hindus and nonreligious people for Christ. We all felt called by God to go, but none of us knew what to expect.

When we arrived, the Indian leader met us and invited us to his home. Over the course of the next few days, he told us about his ministry.

His father, a dynamic leader and speaker, had started the mission in a Hindu-dominated area. One day a Hindu leader came to his father and asked for prayer. Eager to pray with him, hoping he would lead him to Christ, he took him into a private room, knelt down with him, closed his eyes and began to pray. While he was praying, the Hindu man reached into his robe, pulled out a knife and stabbed him repeatedly.

My new friend, hearing his father's screams, ran to help him. He held him in his arms as blood poured out onto the floor of the hut. Three days later, his father died. On his deathbed he said to his son, "Please tell that man that he is forgiven. Care for your mother and carry on this ministry. Do whatever it takes to win people to Christ."

With more courage and faith than most people will ever dream of mustering, this man of God has complied. For over twenty years, he has been working with unbelievable intensity. He has started over a hundred churches and a medical clinic, along with many other kinds of ministries.

Every year, usually in February, he rents a huge park, sets up a stage and a makeshift sound system, puts together some lights with bare wire, and holds evangelistic meetings for a week. He advertises these meetings with posters and through loudspeaker announcements in the town. And people come by the thousands and sit on the ground in front of the stage, men on one side and women and children on the other.

The evening meetings start at six o'clock. For about half an hour they listen to recorded instrumental music, followed by a couple of special musical numbers. Then comes the warm-up sermon. Instructional, practical and relevant to everyday life, its object is to show the listeners that Christianity makes sense.

At about eight o'clock, there are two more musical numbers. Then comes the main message. It is always centered on the person of Jesus Christ. The speaker talks about who Jesus was, what he did, how he died, how his death pays the price for sin, how his resurrection gives power to people who put their faith and trust in him.

From nine o'clock till nine-thirty, listeners—whether Hindu, Muslim or nonreligious—are invited to put their faith in Christ. They are asked to come forward to receive forgiveness, cleansing and eternal life, and then they're challenged to abandon whatever other god or religious system they brought with them to the meeting and to put their faith and trust solely in Jesus.

A Terrifying Assignment in India

From Tuesday through Thursday I had manageable assignments. Either I spoke at a much smaller morning meeting, or I gave the warm-up sermon in the evening. But when Friday came around the leader of the ministry said, "I received a leading from God, and I want you to give the main message tonight." Dumbfounded, I wondered why I hadn't had a similar leading!

The language barrier seemed almost insurmountable, even with a translator. I wasn't familiar with the culture, so I couldn't speak relevantly to the people's situations. I would have a hard time with humor. There were so many unknowns that every time I tried to pray, after thirty seconds I would be stopped by doubt and fear. *What's the use?* I thought. *The barriers are insurmountable.*

Evening came. We took a rickshaw to the park. As we approached, we could hear the first message over the loudspeakers. I had a little time to nurse my paranoia.

We took our seats at the back of the stage. As I looked out, I saw one of the largest seas of faces I have ever seen in my life. One of the Indian leaders poked me and said,

"Twenty thousand here tonight, maybe thirty." With that, any nugget of confidence I may have had departed.

This is going to be a disaster! I thought. *What am I doing here?* I looked over behind the stage and saw the leader of the ministry and several of his trusted leaders on their faces in the dirt praying. *I know what they're praying about,* I thought. *They realize that this American who is going to give the main message is perfectly capable of emptying out the whole park in a matter of minutes!*

I knew that those praying men were living in poverty and fighting unbelievable odds in order to tell God's message. They had given their whole lives so that people caught up in false religious systems could come to know the truth of Jesus Christ. And since these annual meetings were the focal point of their whole year's efforts, I felt sick at heart over the setback their work would suffer because of my inept preaching.

Great Is Thy Faithfulness

At that point the first speaker ended his message. That meant I had about ten minutes left before I would be on the firing line. Moments later, the vocalist from my church stepped up to the microphone to sing. *I probably should support her in prayer,* I thought, *but my turn is next, and when the chips are down it's every man for himself.*

My praying took on new earnestness. *Oh Lord, deliver me. Make it rain. Make me disappear!* The mountain looked so large that I saw no point in asking God to move it. I would be content if it would simply cave in on me and put me out of my misery.

As my pitiful prayers were bouncing around in my doubt-filled mind, I faintly heard the vocalist.

Great is thy faithfulness, O God my Father,
There is no shadow of turning with thee;
Thou changest not, thy compassions they fail not;
As thou hast been thou forever wilt be.
Great is thy faithfulness! Great is thy faithfulness!
Morning by morning new mercies I see;
All I have needed thy hand hath provided—
Great is thy faithfulness, Lord, unto me!

Like me, our singer didn't know the language of her listeners. Therefore, she couldn't just sing a song; it had to be heart-to-heart communication, or nothing would happen. And as she was communicating heart to heart with the thousands of people out beyond the stage, she was also communicating with a faint-hearted, doubt-filled, faith-starved pastor who needed that song a lot more than the crowd did.

Something happened to me as I listened to the lyrics, "Great is *thy* faithfulness." As the words rolled over my mind, it suddenly dawned on me where the focus of my attention had been all day. I was focusing on myself—my language barrier, my cultural confusion, my inexperience, my weakness, my fear of failing, my terror of a crowd that size. I was looking squarely at my mountain, and all I could see was my inability to move it.

My prayers were pitiful because I was looking at my inadequacy instead of God's adequacy!

A Change of Focus

As the song continued, I said to myself, *Wait a minute! Let's change the focus right now. Let's look at God, not at Hybels.*

I didn't have much time, but I started saying very intensely, *I'm praying to the Creator of the world, the King of the universe, the all-powerful, all-knowing, all-faithful God. I'm praying to the God who made the mountains and who can move them if necessary. I'm praying to the God who has always been faithful to me, who has never let me down no matter how frightened I was or how difficult the situation looked. I'm praying to a God who wants to bear fruit through me, and I am going to trust that he is going to use me tonight. Not because of who I am, but because of who he is. He is faithful.*

By the time the song ended, I was a different person inside. I still would have taken a raincheck if one had been offered, but I wasn't panicky anymore. I was willing to proceed because a faithful God was the object of my full attention. When I walked up to the podium with my translator, I prayed a mountain-moving prayer because it was firmly fixed on God's adequacy, not my inadequacy.

I spoke with Spirit-given confidence that night. It was based on God's sufficiency. I told those people that someone had shed his blood to pay for their sins. This someone was not a Buddha, not a Hindu god, not a character in a myth or fairy tale. He was a real human being named Jesus, and he is God's only Son. I told them over and over again, "You matter to him. He shed his blood for the forgiveness of *your* sin, so you could go free if you put your faith and trust in him." As I was speaking, I knew God was working.

I ended the message, and an invitation was given for people to trust Christ. I went back behind the stage, got down on my knees and started praying: "O Lord, I know how these people matter to you. Draw them to yourself."

Hundreds and hundreds of people came forward — Hindus, Muslims, unbelievers of all sizes and shapes, colors and ages. So many came that I thought my heart would burst. I was rejoicing for all the people who came forward and found new life in Christ, and I was also rejoicing because that night God, through prayer, had taken a mountain called *fear* and cast it into the depths of the sea.

That night, I learned that God sees no barriers. God is ready to use me. When I began to focus on God instead of the mountain, he was able to work through me.

Gotta Go Through It

The second principle of mountain-moving faith is this: *God gives us faith as we walk with him.*

An Old Testament story illustrates this principle well. As Joshua 3 opens, the Israelites are camped on the bank of the Jordan River. Forty years earlier, they miraculously escaped from Egypt. For a generation, they have been wandering in a rugged wilderness, all their needs miraculously met by God. Now they are in sight of the Promised Land, Canaan, but they have an enormous problem: a river is directly in their path, and there's no convenient way around it. To make matters worse, it is flood season, and any usual fording places are impassable. The waters are deep and turbulent and menacing.

God could easily make the river subside right before their eyes. He could throw a wide bridge across it. But he doesn't. Instead, he gives Joshua some strange orders that he passes on to the camp.

First, camp officers order the people to keep an eye on the ark of the covenant. As soon as they see the priests carrying it, they are to fall in behind them.

Second, Joshua tells the people to expect amazing things to happen.

Third, Joshua commands the priests to pick up the ark and go stand in the river.

Take That First Step

This will take a bit of courage. Yes, the Lord said he would provide a dry path through the river, but the priests have never seen this happen before (they hadn't even been born when the Red Sea was parted).

Having spent their entire adult lives in the wilderness, the priests are not swimmers. In fact, this is probably the first river they have ever seen close up. Although the Jordan is not the Amazon or the Mississippi, it doesn't look particularly friendly during flood season. And with a few hundred thousand anxious Israelites at their heels, it will be hard to change their minds and turn around if the river keeps on flowing.

In spite of the problems, the priests had faith enough to obey, and this is what happened: "As soon as the priests who carried the ark reached the Jordan and their feet touched the water's edge, the water from upstream stopped flowing. . . . The priests who carried the ark of the covenant of the LORD stood firm on dry ground in the middle of the Jordan, while all Israel passed by until the whole nation had completed the crossing on dry ground" (Joshua 3:15-17).

God didn't give the priests absolute proof or even overwhelming evidence that the waters would part. He did nothing until they put their feet in the water, taking the first step of commitment and obedience. Only then did he stop the flow of the river. In the same way, mountain-moving faith will be given to us as we step out and follow the Lord's direction.

Move Over, Mountain

How do you pray a prayer so filled with faith that it can move a mountain? By shifting the focus from the size of your mountain to the sufficiency of the mountain mover, and by stepping forward in obedience. As you walk with God, your faith will grow, your confidence will increase and your prayer will have power.

While the children of Israel are perched on the edge of the Promised Land, twelve spies go out to survey it. Ten come back saying, "You wouldn't believe the size of the cities, the armies, the giants. We'd better look somewhere else." Two come back saying, "The God who is faithful promised he would give us the land, so let's go in his strength." Ten looked at the size of the mountain and fell back; only two looked at the sufficiency of the mountain mover and wanted to move forward. (Read the story in Numbers 13.)

Israel's warriors are standing on a hill overlooking a battlefield, and the Philistine champion Goliath swaggers out to frighten them. The warriors say, "We're not going down there to fight him. He's nine feet tall. Look at his armor! Look at his spear! I don't want that thing in my ribs." The adolescent shepherd David comes out, surveys the field, and says, "Look at the size of our God. Let me go!" (Read the story in 1 Samuel 17.)

Probably every human being alive is standing in the shadow of at least one mountain that just will not move: a destructive habit, a character flaw, an impossible marriage or work situation, a financial problem, a physical disability. What is your immovable mountain? Have you stood in its shadow for so long that you've grown accustomed to the darkness? Do you end your prayers by thinking, *What's the use?*

I challenge you to shift the focus of your prayer. Don't spend a lot of time describing your mountain to the Lord. He knows what it is. Instead, focus your attention on the mountain mover—his glory, power and faithfulness. Then start walking in faith, following his leading, and watch that mountain step aside.

8

The Hurt
of Unanswered Prayer

Nearly every week someone meets me at the church or calls my office and asks, "Bill, didn't Jesus say, 'Ask and it will be given to you; seek and you will find; knock and the door will be opened to you'?"

Not having been born yesterday, and being fairly confident where conversations that open like that usually go, I sometimes bypass a theological discussion of Jesus' words in Matthew 7:7 and simply ask, "Friend, what prayer have you been praying that you fear God is not answering? Let's get right to the root of the matter." It's amazing how often that response opens the door for an outpouring of honest confusion and frustration.

☐ I've been praying for my husband to stop drinking, and he came home drunk again last night.

☐ I've been praying for a job, but no one wants to hire a fifty-year-old middle manager.

☐ I've been praying for my wife's depression, and now she's threatening suicide.

On and on the lamentations go, week after week, month

after month, year after year. I couldn't begin to count how many people I've counseled about the mystery—or perhaps more accurately, the agony—of unanswered prayer. And the people who suffer most keenly are those who truly believe that prayer moves mountains.

In private counseling sessions with individuals who are troubled because their prayers aren't being answered, I use a little outline I borrowed from a pastor friend of mine:

☐ If the request is wrong, God says, "No."

☐ If the timing is wrong, God says, "Slow."

☐ If you are wrong, God says, "Grow."

☐ But if the request is right, the timing is right and you are right, God says, "Go!"

We'll look at the first two problems—wrong requests and wrong timing—in this chapter, saving the third problem for chapter nine, where we can look at it in some detail.

Inappropriate Requests

First, if the request is wrong, God says, "No." Some prayer requests, no matter how well intentioned, are inappropriate. Jesus' disciples were not immune from making misguided requests. Not even the three who were closest to him—Peter, James and John.

These three famous disciples once accompanied Jesus to the top of a high mountain. Suddenly God's full glory descended upon Jesus, and Moses and Elijah appeared beside him. Beholding God's splendor just a few feet from where they were standing, Peter, James and John dropped back in awe. Then Peter came up with a bright idea. Some believe, loosely translated, his request went like this: "Jesus, let us build shelters up here for you and Moses and Elijah. We'll be happy to stay on the mountain with you and bask in your glory."

Jesus' immediate response was effectively *no:* a thick cloud enveloped them, cutting off further conversation. Jesus and the disciples still had work to do down in the plains where people lived. They couldn't stay on the mountaintop. Peter's request was inappropriate, and Jesus would not grant it. (See the complete story in Matthew 17:1-8; Mark 9:2-8; Luke 9:28-36.)

Another time James and John came with their mother to Jesus, asking if they could reserve the best two seats in his kingdom. It wasn't just a good view they were after; they wanted to be Jesus' chief executive officers. "No, " said Jesus. "You don't know what you're asking. There's going to be a lot of pain and hardship in my kingdom before my glory is revealed. Besides, the places of honor are already reserved." In other words, "Your request is inappropriate, and I will not grant it." (The story is recorded in Matthew 20:20-23; Mark 10:35-40.)

James and John seemed to have a knack for requesting the wrong thing. Sometime after the transfiguration, Jesus and the disciples were denied a travel permit through a Samaritan village. This setback irritated James and John so much that they asked Jesus to destroy the village with fire from heaven. Once again, Jesus denied their request. In fact, he rebuked them for making it. (Luke 9:51-56 tells the story.)

Too Loving to Say Yes

If the disciples were capable of making wrong requests —

requests that were totally self-serving, patently materialistic, shortsighted, immature—so am I and so are you. Fortunately, our God loves us too much to say yes to inappropriate requests. He will answer such prayers, but he will say no. I wouldn't want a God who would do any less than that.

In hindsight, I thank God for saying no to prayers that at the time seemed appropriate. I remember once when my church was looking to fill an important staff position. As a staff we had been praying for years that God would show us the right person to fill the need. Then simultaneously we all thought of an individual who looked custom designed to fill the position. We asked God if this person was the one we were looking for, and we agreed to go ahead and contact him in faith.

The elders commissioned me to meet with the person and ask him to consider joining our staff. I took him to a restaurant, and we enjoyed a good lunch together. The whole time I was praying, "Lord, should I ask him right now? Is this the time? You know how desperately we need a person to lead in this area."

As I was ready to launch into my presentation, it became apparent to me that God was saying, "No—don't ask him." I had no idea why, but by God's grace I decided not to issue the invitation. Toward the end of the lunch, the man said, "Was there anything else you wanted to talk to me about?" I answered, "Not really. It's been great seeing you again." And I went back and told the elders I couldn't present the ministry opportunity to the man.

Six months later we learned that there was deception in the life of that leader. His entire ministry crumbled around him, and even today he is disqualified from service. That could have happened in our congregation, and God could have been dishonored in our midst. When I heard the tragic story, I silently prayed, "Thank you, Jesus, for having enough love and concern for our body and for our elders and for our staff to just say no."

The Importance of Motives

It isn't likely, of course, that any of us would approach God with the intention of making a wrong request. What are some wrong requests we might make without even realizing we are out of line?

The most famous wrong request is this: "O God, please change the other person." Wives make this about husbands, husbands about wives, parents about children, employees about bosses. In fact, any time two or more Christian people have to relate closely to each other, somebody is likely to make this request.

Now it's often perfectly appropriate to pray that someone will change. After all, that's what we do when we pray for conversions, for hearts to be softened, for bad habits or addictions to be broken. But too often the motive behind such a request is not authentic concern for the other person.

A more genuine prayer might be this: "I don't want to face my own shortcomings. I don't want to work on this relationship. I don't want to change at all. Instead, I want the other person to accommodate all my personal needs, so I'm asking you to change him or her." If you pray that kind of prayer, God may say no.

God's Glory or Mine?

There are plenty of other inappropriate, self-serving prayers masquerading as reasonable requests. "Please give me this new account" may be a good request for account executives to make. There's nothing wrong in praying for help in business; we should bring all our concerns to God. But if our motivation is to show off in front of the other sellers, or to get rich in order to live lavishly, or to thumb our noses at supervisors who advised us not to go after the account, it's a wrong request and God is likely to say no.

Or pastors may pray, "O Lord, help our church grow." Surely God would want to honor that request! But if the pastors' real meaning is "I want to be a star with a big church, fancy programs and lots of media coverage, " their requests are wrong.

Likewise, the Christian musicians who pray, "Help my album sell and my concert tour to take shape," may be asking for personal glory, no matter how often they refer to God on-stage. We can fool ourselves into thinking selfish requests are appropriate, but we can't fool God. He knows when our motives are destructive, and he often protects us from them by saying no.

Before bringing a request to the Lord, it's a good idea to ask: If God granted this request,

☐ would it bring glory to him?

☐ would it advance his kingdom?

☐ would it help people?

☐ would it help me to grow spiritually?

By forcing us to look closely at our requests, prayer can purify us. When we conclude that our motives have been wrong, we can say, "Lord, forgive me. Help me grow. Help me present requests that are in line with your will."

If you have been praying diligently about a matter and have sensed resistance from heaven, I challenge you to review your request. It may be the problem. Maybe your request is a cop-out on your part, an unwillingness to face the real issue. Maybe it is destructive in ways you don't understand. Maybe it is self-serving, shortsighted or too small. God may have something better in mind. Whatever the reason, if the request is wrong, God says, "No! "

Sometimes the reason for our request is not wrong, but in the infinite mystery of things, the outcome still seems to be "No." Every day, godly people are stricken with dreaded deadly diseases. Praying parents die without having seen their wayward children return to the fold. Unspeakable tragedies afflict believers and nonbelievers alike. The righteous suffer and the innocent perish. Unsuspecting worshipers are killed without cause; a tower topples onto eighteen Jews, crushing them indiscriminately (Luke 13:1-4). The apostle James is beheaded while Peter is miraculously delivered (Acts 12). The apostle Paul suffers all his life from a thorn in the flesh and finally dies under the ax of the Roman executioner. Many Christians sense that God hears and empathizes with their prayers, but some requests remain unanswered. Why would an all-loving, all-powerful God deny valid requests from faithful believers?

We need to remember that despite the victory God has achieved over Satan in the ministry and resurrection of Christ, everything is not yet submitted to God. The enemy is still active. His years are counted and his end is sure. But in the meantime, he still remains the prince of this world, and he opposes the ways of God. He causes much suffering, and he often seems to have the upper hand.

However, God will have the final say, and he will assert his universal sovereignty in salvation and judgment at Christ's second coming. Because of this ultimate victory, Christians have the assurance that those very prayers which remained unanswered in this life will receive spectacular vindication in eternity. Then, God "will wipe away every tear from their eyes. There will be no more death or mourning or crying or pain, for the old order of things has passed away." (Revelation 21:4).

Not Yet

If the timing is wrong, God says, "Slow." For most of us, this does not feel much better than *no*.

We live in an instant society, always trying to do everything faster. Freeways and supermarkets have express lanes; film companies promise prints in one hour; and we think our computers need upgrading if they make us wait five seconds. That explains why people have said to me, "I don't know what to think. I've been praying for something for three days now, and God hasn't done a thing about it."

Parents know that children rank the words *not yet* as nearly the most awful in the English language, second only to the word *no*. You're leaving on a five-hundred-mile trip in the car. You're fifteen miles from home, and you slow down for a toll booth. Voices from the back seat ask, "Are we there yet?" "Not yet," you say, and the groans and complaints begin.

"My birthday's tomorrow. May I open my presents to-night? It's close enough."

"All the other fourth-graders wear makeup to school. May I?"

"Now that I'm fourteen, will you teach me to drive?"

How children hate to hear the answer "Not yet." And there's an impatient child in all of us, a child who wants God to meet every need, grant every request, move every mountain right now, if not yesterday. When the all-knowing, all-wise, loving heavenly Father deems it best to say, "Not yet, " what is our mature adult response? "But God, you don't understand. I want it right now. Not three years from now. Not three months from now. Not three days from now. Read my lips as I pray—I want it *now!*"

Trusting the Father

God, however, is no more intimidated by childish demands for instant gratification than wise parents are. He simply shakes his head at our immaturity and says, "Kick and scream if you must, but you can't have what you want yet. Trust me. I know what I'm doing. I have my reasons."

Be wary of insisting that you know better than God about when a prayer request should be granted. God's delays are not necessarily denials. He has reasons for his *not yets.*

Sometimes God delays in order to test our faith. Do we think of him as a celestial vending machine that we should kick if we don't get an instant response? Or do we relate to him as a loving Father who will give us what we need when we need it? Can we trust him even if we don't see immediate results?

Sometimes God delays so that we can modify our requests. Over times we may see that the original request wasn't quite legitimate. As we understand the situation better, we may want to modify it to make it more in line with God's will.

Sometimes God delays so that we can develop character qualities such as endurance, trust, patience and submission—qualities that come only when we wait patiently and trust in his timing. A lot of spiritual gains come through pain, hurt, struggle, confusion and disappointment. If we had our way, though, how long would any of us put up with these character builders without asking God to remove them?

We may not be able to see the reasons for the delay, but that isn't surprising. As God says through the prophet Isaiah, "My thoughts are not your thoughts, neither are your ways my ways. . . . As the heavens are higher than the earth, so are my ways higher than your ways and my thoughts than your thoughts"(Isaiah 55:8-9). We are the creatures; God is the Creator. He knows what timing is best.

How often I have waited for months and even years for my prayers to be answered! Frequently I have wondered if God was saying, "No," only to find out later that he was saying, "Not yet," so that he could orchestrate a greater miracle than I had the faith to pray for in the beginning. When the results are in, God's wisdom is clear, and I am glad I waited patiently for it to be revealed.

My Own Worst Problem

There is a third reason our prayers may not be answered. It

is possible that something is wrong in our lives, that we have set up some barrier between ourselves and God.

Imagine you've been on a vacation for two or three weeks. You come back and discover that the person you hired to mow your lawn went to the hospital the day after you left and has been in traction ever since. Your lawn is about eight inches high, and you know your Kmart Eclipse is not going to handle it.

Fortunately your neighbor has a John Deere riding mower that will cut anything, and he has often said to you, "Look, if you ever get in a jam, you can use my mower." You decide to take him up on his offer.

On the way to his house, as you're mentally rehearsing your request, your neighbor's little dachshund waddles up and starts bothering your pant legs. Now, you hate dachshunds, especially this one. It howls, it messes on your lawn, and it snaps at you—which is exactly what it's doing right now. You can hardly put one foot in front of the other without getting bitten or tripped.

Exasperated, you give the little fellow a sly, swift kick. Then you look up and see your neighbor standing on his front porch, arms folded, looking straight at you. Is it a good moment to ask for the lawn mower? Or is there something you need to clear up before asking for favors?

God repeatedly invites us to come to him with all our needs. He offers us free access to all his resources. But some of us have a few things we need to clear up before taking him up on his offer.

In the next chapter we'll look at six "prayer busters"— actions and attitudes that can block our access to God.

9

Prayer Busters

If someone asked you what most motivates you to develop your personal prayer life, how would you answer? What drives you to your knees and makes you want to pray more? What makes your prayers more fervent?

For me, the greatest prayer motivator is *answered prayer.*

When I pray about a sermon and God answers by giving mean insight from his Word, a way of organizing the material, an apt illustration or a sense of his power as I give the message, I'm motivated to pray about the next sermon I work on.

When I pray for someone who doesn't know the Lord and one day the person calls me up and says, "I'm a member of the family now—I've given my life to Christ," I'm motivated to continue praying for the other seeking people on my list.

When I pray over a difficult decision and then get a sense of God's leading, follow his direction and see by hindsight that I made the best possible choice, I'm motivated to pray about all the decisions that come my way.

And when I pray about a need that cannot be met by any human means and God meets it through his miracle-working power, I'm motivated to get down on my knees and pray for all kinds of needs, whether personal, ministry related or global.

Me, a Problem?

Answered prayer really motivates me. It makes me feel like Moses on the mountain with his arms upraised, directing the battle through his prayers. When my prayers have that kind of demonstrable results, it's fun to pray.

By contrast, my prayer life takes a dive when I'm praying diligently, fervently and trustingly without seeming to make any difference. Nothing is more devitalizing than a string of unanswered prayers. You call heaven, and no one seems to be home. The troops are getting massacred before your eyes, and you feel like lowering your arms and saying, "What's the use?"

For each unanswered prayer, it's important to check out three possible hindrances. In the last chapter we looked at two major reasons prayers go unanswered: the request may be inappropriate, and the timing may be off. If you're faced with a long list of unanswered prayers, however, you may want to pay special attention to the third category: there may be a problem in the life of the person who is praying.

It's unlikely that *all* your requests are inappropriate, even though some may very well be. It's unlikely that your timing is *always* off, even though sometimes you may push ahead of God. It's more likely that some malfunction in your life is blocking your prayers, even the appropriate, well-timed ones.

And yet when prayers are not answered, most people want to know what's wrong with God. This is a normal human response. It's a lot easier to blame God than to look in the mirror and say, "Maybe I'm the problem." In fact, of the thousands of people I've counseled about the mystery of unanswered prayer, only a handful have asked, "Do you think I might be the obstacle to the miracle I'm praying for?"

I once asked a group of church leaders to list biblical reasons for unanswered prayer. Most of the reasons they put down were in this third category—problems in the life of the praying person. I call these reasons *prayer busters*. Let's look at some of the important ones.

Everything But Prayer

The most common cause of unanswered prayer is *prayerlessness*. As James 4:2 says, "You do not have, because you do not ask God."

Be honest with yourself: how often does something like this happen? You decide to pray about something. You add it to your prayer list or tell a friend that you are praying about it, and you almost do. But even though you think about it from time to time, you hardly pray about it at all. Why isn't God answering your prayer? Because you haven't yet prayed purposefully, fervently or expectantly.

People often tell me how they have attempted to address a pressing need. They have gone to counselors, read self-help books, claimed biblical promises, practiced self-discipline, confided in Christian friends, practiced assertiveness or submission or self-denial or positive thinking, even read books about prayer—and their need is still not met.

I say to these people, "Look me right in the eye and tell me if you've prayed about this fervently and regularly over an extended period of time."

Usually they shift from one foot to another, look down and mumble, "Well, uh, you know, uh, I guess not."

I understand all too well. I have to admit I'm often a member of the club whose motto is "When all else fails, pray." Why pray when I can worry? Why pray when I can work myself to death trying to get what I need without help? Why pray when I can go without?

Regular, Earnest and Persistent

When was the last time you prayed diligently over a period of time

☐ for your spouse, your parents, your children?

☐ for someone to come to know Christ?

☐ for peace in the war-torn parts of our world?

☐ that God's power would cause a revolution in your church?

☐ that God would use you to work for his glory?

In 1978 I traveled to Korea to visit the world's largest church. At that time every Friday night from eight o'clock until seven o'clock Saturday morning, ten thousand people gathered in an auditorium and prayed that God would take the church's ministry by storm. Every Saturday several thousand people went to a mountain they call Prayer Mountain, sat in its many caves and prayed that God would work in a supernatural way.

In 1978 the church had 100,000 members. Some people might have thought it was large enough, but its members had a vision. Ten prayer-filled years later, the church membership was up to 450,000. Today there are over one million members. When we work, we work; when we pray, God works!

I've heard it said that if you bring a thimble to God, he'll fill it. If you bring a bucket to God, he'll fill that. If you bring a five-hundred-gallon barrel to God, he'll fill that too. Are you expecting God to fill your needs? Are you asking him to do so—regularly, earnestly, persistently?

Contaminated by Cheating

The second reason for unanswered prayer is the most obvious. *Unconfessed sin* cuts off our communication with the Father. As Isaiah 59:2 says, "Your iniquities have separated you from your God; your sins have hidden his face from you, so that he will not hear."

I used to race motorcycles. A motorcycle is a rugged machine that can take incredible abuse, but its fuel has to be pure. At refueling time, I would pour the fuel through a filter or a handkerchief to be sure no contaminants could prevent the engine from running at its full potential. Any speck of dirt could cause a loss of power. Likewise, if you let even a little sin into your heart, it's going to contaminate your prayers. Your Christian life will not achieve its full potential.

God expects us to maintain strict personal integrity. He expects us to show thoughtfulness and love toward others and to maintain a relationship with him. "What does the

Lord require of you? To act justly and to love mercy and to walk humbly with your God" (Micah 6:8). If we refuse to do these things, we are presumptuous to expect God to answer our prayers. (In the next chapter, I'll discuss the guilt of unconfessed sin in more detail.)

If you're tolerating sin in your life, don't waste your breath praying unless it's a prayer of confession. Receive the Lord's forgiveness, and then he will listen when you pour out your heart to him.

Broken Relationships

The third prayer buster is *unresolved relational conflict.* Matthew 5:23-24 says, "If you are offering your gift at the altar and there remember that your brother has something against you, leave your gift there in front of the altar. First go and be reconciled to your brother; then come and offer your gift."

First Peter 3:7 extends this principle: "Husbands, . . . be considerate as you live with your wives, and treat them with respect as the weaker partner and as heirs with you of the gracious gift of life, so that nothing will hinder your prayers."

Most of us grossly underestimate how committed God is to building and maintaining a loving community, a family. He adopts us into his family, and he wants us to carry our relationship with him into our relationships with others. If we do good to our brothers and sisters, it is like doing good to Jesus himself (Matthew 25:31-46). Since God has forgiven us, we should forgive others (Ephesians 4:32; Colossians 3:13).

There's no point in trying to pray if we are engaged in ongoing conflict with a family member, a coworker, a neighbor, a friend. "Anyone who claims to be in the light but hates his brother is still in the darkness" (1 John 2:9). God will listen when you come out into the light, confess the sins that drove you and the other person apart and attempt to mend the relationship.

Of course it isn't always possible to make amends. Romans 12:18 says, "If it is possible, as far as it depends on you, live at peace with everyone." Sometimes the other person would rather continue the warfare than accept your apology. If this happens, look deep into your heart. Have you sincerely tried to restore the relationship, or are you holding something back? Do you really want restoration, or would you rather blame the other person and let the rupture continue? If your attempts have been wholehearted and honest, God will not let the broken relationship stand in the way of your prayers. But if your reconciliation attempts have been halfhearted and self-serving, try again — this time for real.

Dear Santa Claus

Selfishness is the fourth prayer buster. "When you ask, you do not receive, because you ask with wrong motives, that you may spend what you get on your pleasures" (James 4:3). Many of the inappropriate requests we looked at in the last chapter are wrong because they are selfish. Selfishness in the heart is a very common barrier between the Christian and God.

How would you feel if your prayer requests were made public, displayed on a billboard or marquee? "Dear Lord, make me famous. Make me rich. Make sure I have a good time. Make all my dreams come true."

When I began to study prayer, I was devastated over this point. I went over my usual prayers and had to face up to a lot of ugly covetousness. There was grand confusion between wants and needs, rights and favors, justice and grace, convenience and conformity to Christ.

I found that I'd been saying, in effect, "Keep me from trial or tragedy or pain or anything that would make me really grow and become a man of God. Just give me a convenient, happy, satisfying, problem-free life."

When Jesus prayed the model prayer we call the Lord's Prayer, his first requests were that God's name be reverenced, that his kingdom come, that his will be done. That doesn't sound much like the self-centered, shortsighted prayers I'd been saying.

I'd been wondering why my prayers were infrequently answered. When I took a good look at what I'd been praying for, I understood. If God had granted such patently selfish requests, I would quickly be spiritually destroyed.

Hearing the Cry of the Poor

The fifth prayer buster is *uncaring attitudes*. Proverbs 21:13 says, "If you close your ear to the cry of the poor, you will cry out and not be heard" (NRSV).

A beautiful passage in the Old Testament is about this prayer buster. The Israelites were wondering why God was not answering their prayers. They had even fasted and humbled themselves—and he still did not listen. Here is what he told them through his prophet:

On the day of your fasting, you do as you please and exploit all your workers. . . . You cannot fast as you do today and expect your voice to be heard on high. . . . Is not this the kind of fasting I have chosen: to loose the chains of injustice and untie the cords of the yoke, to set the oppressed free and break every yoke? Is it not to share your food with the hungry and to provide the poor wanderer with shelter—when you see the naked, to clothe him, and not to turn away from your own flesh and blood? . . . Then you will call, and the LORD will answer; you will cry for help, and he will say: Here am I." (Isaiah 58:3-9)

God is committed to developing a people who will reflect his character in this world, and his character always expresses concern and compassion for the afflicted.

I once saw a cartoon picturing hundreds and hundreds of people lined up as far back as the eye can see. Each person was thinking the same thing: *What can I do? I'm just one person.*

As just one person, you may not be able to change the world. You can, however, look for a small way to care. Perhaps your church works with a food pantry or prison ministry. Maybe your skills could make a small difference in today's evils of unemployment, illiteracy, child abuse, alcoholism or suicide. If your ear is open to the afflicted, God will keep his ear open to you.

A God Who Is Able

Inadequate faith is the final prayer buster. "If any of you is lacking in wisdom, ask God, who gives to all generously and ungrudgingly, and it will be given to you. But ask in faith, never doubting, for the one who doubts is like a wave of the sea, driven and tossed by the wind; for the doubter, being double-minded and unstable in every way, must not expect to receive anything from the Lord" (James 1:5-8 NRSV).

Is God able? Is he omnipotent? If you don't own that doctrine, you might as well pitch prayer. If your prayers have clouds of doubt hanging over them, they won't get anywhere.

Before getting down on your knees, go to Scripture and look at what God has done for his people. Then review his track record in your own life, looking for evidence of his power, his faithfulness, his provision. Tune your mind properly so that when you finally pray, it will be to a God who is able.

The more you are convinced of God's ability, the more he demonstrates his ability to you. Jesus never tells his followers to throw wishes heavenward. Instead he says, "I tell you the truth, if anyone says to this mountain, 'Go, throw yourself into the sea,' and does not doubt in his heart but believes that what he says will happen, it will be done for him" (Mark 11:23). When you pray, plan on seeing a mighty demonstration of God's power.

God Says, "Go!"

If the truth were known, often you and I are the only obstacles standing in the way of our receiving a desperately needed miracle. Our requests may be right. The timing may not be a problem. But when our lives are wrong God says, "Before I grant your request, I want you to grow. Put that sin away. Change your attitude. Stop that practice, end that pattern, get off that merry-go-round, reconcile that relationship, soften up your spirit, repent, receive forgiveness. Grow—and I'll 'throw open the floodgates of heaven and pour out so much blessing that you will not have room enough for it'" (Malachi 3:10).

Probably none of us can understand how much God wants to change that impossible circumstance, touch that untouchable person, move that immovable mountain in our lives. We matter to him, and he wants to meet our needs and grant our requests if we will free him to do it. When our request is right, when the timing is right and when the person is right, God says, "Go!"

Nothing motivates people to develop their prayer lives more than answered prayers. And once the prayer busters are dealt with and dispatched, the way is clear for God to answer one prayer after another.

10

Cooling Off on Prayer

A few months ago I was talking with some embarrassed Christians. They used to have a good prayer life, they told me. But things had changed. They no longer prayed like they once did, and they felt ashamed. One man described it like this:

"When I was a brand-new believer, the thought of talking with the God of the universe, the thought of God listening to me—caring about me, responding to my concerns—it was so overwhelming I could barely take it in.

"Once I learned I could actually do this, I began to pray all day. I prayed when I got up. I prayed at the breakfast table. I prayed in the car on the way to work. I prayed at my desk, with friends over the telephone, at lunch, with my family at dinner, with my kids when I put them to bed. I prayed with my small group. I loved it when we prayed at church.

"I just prayed all the time, and it brought me such joy.

God was answering my prayers. My life was changing. Other people's lives were changing. It was wonderful."

"What happened?" I asked.

"I don't know," the man said. "I honestly don't know. The whole deal just cooled off." Then he said with great sadness, "I don't pray much at all anymore."

The Prayerless Season

I knew where those people were coming from. "Almost every follower of Jesus Christ at some time has experienced exactly what you describe," I said. "I know I have."

When I look back over the years of my spiritual life, I see certain seasons where I prayed eagerly and often. I was filled with joy and the anticipation of God's blessings. Supernatural things happened in my life, in the lives of people I prayed for and in the church.

And then, for who knows what reason, my prayer life would begin to wind down until I had almost given up on praying. I would still pray at meals and at church functions, of course, but not a whole lot more than that. Prayer would seem dry, tedious and pointless. This prayerless season could last for weeks or even months.

And then suddenly God's power would flood into my life again, just as before. Once again I would delight in coming into God's presence. Once again I would pray often and with results. Until the fade began again, as it always did.

What causes these ups and downs in our prayer life? Why do we lose interest in prayer? Why do we stop praying?

One reason we stop praying or let our prayer lives fade is that we are too comfortable. It's human nature.

When the storms rage and the winds howl and the waves break over the deck, everyone on board is praying like crazy. When the dreaded phone call comes in the middle of the night, when the doctor says it doesn't look good, or when your spouse says someone else is looking mighty attractive, prayer is almost second nature. In difficult situations like those, almost everyone prays—fervently, repeatedly, hopefully, even desperately.

And then the storm passes, the seas settle down, the wind diminishes, and God proves himself faithful yet one more time. A big part of our motivation to pray subsides, and the great prayer fade begins.

Forgetting God

Understandably, this affects the heart of God. He is not beyond feeling used by his children. Especially when we act like college kids who phone home—collect—only when their money runs low.

There is a sad theme running through the Old Testament. God blesses his children, and they forget him. He blesses them again, and they forget him again. They get in big trouble and beg for help, and God comes through with an eleventh-hour rescue. Yet they forget him once again.

Read, for example, the sad litany in Psalm 78. Though God gave Israel the law, divided the sea so they could pass through, guided them through the desert, gave them miraculous food and water, and drove back their enemies, "again and again they put God to the test; . . . they did not remember his power" (vv. 41-42).

Or in Psalm 106:

When our fathers were in Egypt,
   they gave no thought to your miracles;
they did not remember your many kindnesses,
   and they rebelled by the sea, the Red Sea.
Yet he saved them for his name's sake,
   to make his mighty power known.
He rebuked the Red Sea, and it dried up;
   he led them through the depths as through a desert.
He saved them from the hand of the foe;
   from the hand of the enemy he redeemed them.
The waters covered their adversaries;
   not one of them survived.
Then they believed his promises
   and sang his praise.

But they soon forgot what he had done
   and did not wait for his counsel. (vv. 7-13)

Sadly, says the psalmist, "we have sinned, even as our fathers did" (v. 6). We don't want to forget God. We want our prayer lives to be consistent. How can we stay mindful of God's goodness? How can we remember to pray?

A Daily Rhythm

We can remember to pray the same way we remember anything else that matters to us—by writing prayer into our daily schedule. As we noted in chapter five, Jesus simply assumed that his followers would make time for prayer. If we find we are praying less and less, it may be because we have never made prayer a fixed part of our everyday routine.

Some people have a prayer time even before they kick off the covers in the morning. Others pray over coffee, or at lunch, or right after work or school, or after dinner, or just before bedtime. The time of day we choose for prayer doesn't matter, so long as we keep it faithfully. Prayer needs to be part of the rhythm of our daily lives.

Choose a time when you are usually undisturbed, when you can shut the world out and tune in to God. At the same time, choose a place that can be your refuge, your sanctuary, while you are sitting in God's presence.

The people I know who pray fervently and joyfully and consistently can usually describe the physical environment in which they pray daily. I know a man who prays on the commuter train five days a week. He gets on at the Palatine station and prays all the way into Chicago. That's forty minutes if he catches the express and one hour otherwise. He says his seat on the train is a holy place for him.

I know someone who prays in the corner booth of a restaurant before work every day, someone who prays while sitting by a sliding-glass door overlooking a garden, someone who writes out her prayers on the computer in her home office. Any place can become a place of prayer. What is important, if we want to remember to pray, is to establish a particular place and a particular time for our meetings with the Lord.

Old-Fashioned Sin

But for many of us, the problem with prayer is not a lack of time or place. We have a prayer place, and we used to go there regularly. Somehow we just don't feel like going there anymore. We are no longer eager to pray.

If that describes our feelings, we may be suffering from guilt or shame. Something we have done—or are currently doing—may be standing between us and God.

Sometimes when I'm trying to help someone understand why they don't pray anymore, I say, "Let's just backtrack. Do you know when you started feeling this way? What else was happening in your life at that time?"

People who are honest and self-aware often say something like this: "Well, you know, it was back when I was partying pretty heavily, and I started running around a lot and letting my life get a little out of control."

Someone else will say, "It was when things got really busy at work and greed got its hooks in me, and making money started to be the driving force in my life."

"I think it was when I was getting some counseling, and it was helping me at first. But then instead of facing my problems I got all absorbed in myself, and before you know it I became the center of my universe. I pushed God off to the side."

"It must have been back when I moved in with my boyfriend."

I have to tell these people that, whatever the details, old-fashioned sin is plenty strong enough to create an ever-widening gap in our relationship with God. The wider the gap, the less likely we are to pray. And the less we pray, the wider the gap becomes.

Despising God's Name

I remember a time when I was coloring outside the lines. I

knew I was sinning, but I was still wondering why my early-morning prayer times in my office seemed so cold and mechanical. I had a regular prayer time and a regular prayer place; I just didn't want to get into a deep discussion with God.

Then I read God's words in the book of Malachi. " 'Where is the respect due me?' says the LORD Almighty. 'It is you, O priests, who despise my name.' But you ask, 'How have we despised your name?' "

Lots of ways, God says through Malachi. Let me name a few.

You have been *cheating God.* Despite God's clear instructions to offer only the best animals as sacrifices to the Lord, Israelites were taking their prize animals to market where they could get top dollar for them. Then they took the worthless animals—the blind, the lame, the ready to die—and brought them to God's altar (Malachi 1:7-8).

You have also been *cheating the poor*—paying absurdly low wages, making life economically impossible for single mothers and treating illegal immigrants unjustly (Malachi 3:5).

In addition, you have been *cheating your families.* Divorce was rampant. "You weep and wail because [the Lord] no longer pays attention to your offerings or accepts them with pleasure from your hands. You ask, 'Why?' It is because the LORD is acting as the witness between you and the wife of your youth, because you have broken faith with her, though she is your partner, the wife of your marriage covenant" (2:13-14).

Through Malachi God exclaimed, "After cheating me, the oppressed among you and even your own families, you have the audacity to ask for my blessing? You blatantly sin against me and then have the gall to ask for favors? You rebel against me and then expect me not to be affected by your disobedience? Excuse me, but I am deeply affected. Your sin breaks my heart. It feels like betrayal."

If we do not live in submission to God, we lose the sense of warmth and closeness with him. We may feel nostalgic about the prayer times we used to have, but we've put up a sin barrier that will have to come down before we can enjoy a loving relationship with him again. We can have no deep, ongoing fellowship with God unless we obey him—totally.

Pulling Down the Barrier

The amazing thing is that God himself wants to pull down the barrier that has come between us.

The Scriptures tell us that the God we have sinned against, the God we have shaken our fist at, holds out his arms to us and says, "Come on back. You don't want to live that kind of life, do you? You don't want to go where that path leads. Admit your sin. Tell me you're fouled up. Agree with me that you're on the wrong track. Come on back, and we'll relate closely again. Once again your prayers will be rich and real. We'll walk together again."

"Come now, let us reason together," says the Lord.
"Though your sins are like scarlet,
  they shall be as white as snow;
though they are red as crimson,
  they shall be like wool." (Isaiah 1:18)

The good news is that you can come back into fellowship with the Father right now. You can say a prayer of repentance like this: "God, I'm sorry for ____. Please forgive me. I want to turn from this, and I want to come back into relationship with you."

When you pray that prayer, God will restore you. You'll pray a different kind of prayer after that. You'll be back on track again.

Is God Deaf?

Perhaps you have made room for prayer in your daily schedule, and you are unaware of any sin coming between you and God. All the same, you know you are drifting away from him. You are about to give up on prayer, because you are discouraged. Disillusioned. Or even despairing.

You prayed fervently that your dad would survive the surgery—but he didn't.

You prayed that your son and daughter-in-law would reconcile and stay married—but they wouldn't.

You prayed that your business would withstand a new competition—but it couldn't.

You know that your sins are confessed, and you are trying to lead an ethical life. Your requests are not selfish. And now that your dad has died, your kids are divorced or your business is defunct, God can't be telling you to wait. It's too late for that.

Apparently prayer just doesn't work. Why waste your breath? If heaven doesn't listen, if God doesn't care or if God lacks the power to change things, why pray? Better to face reality and stop kidding yourself.

If you've ever had a crushing disappointment that prayer did not fix, and if you're an honest Christ-follower, you have asked yourself these questions. I do not have a pat answer for you. Some things will never be clear this side of eternity. "We live by faith," says the apostle Paul, "not by sight" (2 Corinthians 5:7).

But I can tell you what Jesus said to his disciples when they felt discouraged. "Jesus told . . . them that they should always pray and not give up," Luke reports. After giving them a parable to illustrate his point, Jesus asked, "Will not God bring about justice for his chosen ones, who cry out to him day and night? Will he keep putting them off? I tell you, he will see that they get justice, and quickly" (Luke 18:1, 7-8).

I plead with you, Jesus says, not to lose heart. Keep on praying. The Father does listen. He hears every prayer we pray. He cares deeply about everything that affects us. He has unlimited power to bring to bear on whatever is causing our concern. True, he doesn't answer every prayer the way we fallible humans wish he would. But he wants us to endure. He loves our company. He is eager to do whatever is best for us.

"I Kept On Praying"
Some years ago we had a baptism Sunday where many people publicly affirmed their decision to follow Christ. I thought my heart would explode for joy. Afterward, in the stairwell, I bumped into a woman who was crying. I couldn't understand how anyone could weep after such a celebration, so I stopped and asked her if she was all right.

"No," she said, "I'm struggling. My mother was baptized today."

This is a problem? I thought.

"I prayed for her every day for twenty years," the woman said, and then she started crying again.

"You're going to have to help me understand this," I said.

"I'm crying," the woman replied, "because I came so close—*so close*—to giving up on her. I mean, after five years I said, *Who needs this? God isn't listening.* After ten years I said, *Why am I wasting my breath?* After fifteen years I said, *This is absurd.* After nineteen years I said, *I'm just a fool.* But I guess I just kept praying, even though my faith was weak. I kept praying, and she gave her life to Christ, and she was baptized today."

The woman paused and looked me in the eye. "I will never doubt the power of prayer again," she said.

11

Slowing Down to Pray

We've looked at several important aspects of prayer: God's gracious invitation for us to come to him as to a father; his incredible power to do more than we ever dream of asking; the habits and attitudes Jesus said we must cultivate in order to pray effectively; the categories we need to be sure to include in our prayers; the reasons our prayers are not always answered the way we wish; and some reasons our prayer lives dry up from time to time.

This information about prayer is important, but it will do us no good if we never slow down long enough to pray. And most of us are far too busy for our spiritual health.

Rev That Engine

If we are involved in the marketplace, we are trained to believe that time is money. That's why we talk about managing time, using it efficiently and profitably, and—as a result of our concern—dealing with time pressures.

Cram more in. Start earlier. Work later. Take work home. Use a laptop on the commuter train. Phone clients while you drive. Check your e-mail while you fly. Schedule breakfasts, lunches and dinners for profit. Performance, performance, performance—it's the key to promotion, to compensation increase, to power.

If an ordinary car engine turns four thousand revolutions per minute, some racing motors can turn up to ten thousand. The marketplace mentality says, "Rev that engine up to ten thousand as soon as you get up in the morning, and keep it there until you collapse in the sack at night."

Getting caught up in that intense pace can be rewarding! It's exciting when the adrenaline starts to flow and you get on a roll, when your motor starts racing faster and faster. But it leaves precious little time for quiet moments with God.

You don't have to be in business to be overcommitted. Women with small children know what it means to do ten thousand rpms all day long. Almost every minute of every day is consumed by those little creatures who pull on your pant legs, color on your walls, track mud on your carpet, throw food on your floor and then have the audacity to fuss in the middle of the night.

The pace of single working parents is double or triple that of the rest of us. It is incomprehensible to me how they can meet the incessant demands of work all day and then go home to face the even more incessant demands of their children, with no time out.

I see pastors, elders and church board members operating at the same relentless pace as everyone else. Never a dull moment; never a reflective moment either. Frightened, I ask myself, *Where does the still, small voice of God fit into our hectic lives? When do we allow him to lead and guide and correct and affirm? And if this seldom or never happens, how can we lead truly authentic Christian lives?*

The Authentic Christian

Authentic Christianity is not learning a set of doctrines and then stepping in cadence with people all marching the same way. It is not simply humanitarian service to the less fortunate. It is a walk—a supernatural walk with a living, dynamic, communicating God. Thus the heart and soul of the Christian life is learning to hear God's voice and developing the courage to do what he tells us to do.

Authentic Christians are persons who stand apart from others, even other Christians, as though listening to a different drummer. Their character seems deeper, their ideas fresher, their spirit softer, their courage greater, their leadership stronger, their concerns wider, their compassion more genuine, their convictions more concrete. They are joyful in spite of difficult circumstances and show wisdom beyond their years.

Authentic Christians are full of surprises. You think you have them neatly boxed, but they turn out to be unpredictable. When you are around them, you feel slightly off balance because you don't know what to expect next. Over time, though, you realize that their unexpected ideas and actions can be trusted.

That's because authentic Christians have strong relationships with the Lord—relationships that are renewed every day. As the psalmist said of godly people, "Their delight is in the law of the LORD, and on his law they meditate day and night. They are like trees planted by streams of water, which yield their fruit in its season and their leaves do not wither" (Psalm 1:2-3 NRSV).

Embarrassingly few Christians ever reach this level of authenticity; most Christians are just too busy. And the archenemy of spiritual authenticity is busyness, which is closely tied to something the Bible calls *worldliness*—getting caught up with this society's agenda, objectives and activities to the neglect of walking with God.

Any way you cut it, a key ingredient in authentic Christianity is time. Not leftover time, not throwaway time, but quality time. Time for contemplation, meditation and reflection. Unhurried, uninterrupted time.

A Commitment to Slow Down

An authentic marriage requires the same kind of time. Many marriages are superficial. The husband gets all wrapped up in his job, hoping to shore up his sagging self-esteem by being impressive at work. The wife is wrapped up in the kids, and she may have a job as well. And so they pass each other in the driveway, the hallway and the walk-in closet. They sleep in the same bed and occasionally sit at the same table, but there's not much intimacy between them. They are cohabiting, but they are not nurturing one another. They are not involved in a vital, refreshing, authentic relationship.

Most couples settle for merely cohabiting. A few courageous couples, however, insist on more. Realizing it won't be easy, they nevertheless decide to fight for an authentic marriage. They know it will take time: they may have to give up activities that have been important to them. They know it may require some practical vehicle to help them make the change: setting a date night, taking evening walks, tossing out the TV, sitting at the table and talking to each other after dinner. They tear up their schedules if necessary and start from scratch, because the results are worth it.

Believers in Christ sometimes come to the same point in their relationships with God. "Choked by life's worries, riches and pleasures" (Luke 8:14), they realize they are no longer growing and maturing. Their walk with Jesus has slowed to a crawl or stopped altogether.

If this has happened to you, one day you may have to say, "That's it! I am not going to go through the motions of being a Christian anymore. I am not going to put my Christian life on autopilot, go through meaningless prayers and page through a Bible that I don't let saturate my life. I'm not going to play half-way games anymore. I'm going to pay whatever price it takes for an authentic walk with Jesus Christ."

Christians who make that commitment know that time is required. Something good is going to have to give way. Some practical vehicle will have to be employed to get the rpms down from ten thousand to five thousand to five hundred, where they can be at peace with God and be in a condition to hear what the Lord is saying.

Nobody ever said the Christian walk is easy. But is anything in this world of greater or more lasting importance?

RPM Reduction

I want to offer you a practical, tested, guaranteed rpm-reduction approach that will help you slow your life down so that you can stop playing games and begin leading an authentic Christian life. It's a three-step program that really works.

To start, I'm going to describe a vehicle that may seem out of place in a book about prayer, but in reality is a very important first step. If your life is rushing in many directions at once, you are incapable of the kind of deep, unhurried prayer vital to the Christian walk. By using this vehicle, you can begin to learn to "be still, and know" that God is God (Psalm 46:10).

This first step toward rpm reduction is called *journaling*. For a long time I didn't know what the word meant. When it was explained to me, I didn't like what I heard.

Journaling (an invented word that you won't find in a dictionary) means keeping a journal—in this case, a spiritual journal. It involves writing down your experiences, observations and reflections; looking behind the events of the day for their hidden meanings; recording ideas as they come to you.

When I first came into contact with journaling, I had visions of people who would spend hours and hours in the middle of the day just letting their stream of consciousness flow all over endless reams of paper. I thought to myself, *Anyone who has time to do that kind of thing is not my kind of person. Don't people have anything better to do with their time?*

But over the years, I found myself drawn to the writings

of a wide variety of people—mystics, Puritans, contemporary authors rich in their devotional handling of Scripture—who seemed to have one thing in common: most of them journaled.

In addition, I began to discover something about certain people in my church and around the country whose ministries and character I deeply respect. Most of them journal too. And yet I knew these people did not climb into ivory towers for the better part of the day.

Practical Journaling

Then I read *Ordering Your Private World* by Gordon MacDonald. MacDonald suggested journaling, but with a different twist.

Go to a drugstore, he said, and buy a spiral notebook. Plan to write in this notebook every day, but restrict yourself to one page. Every day when you open to the next blank sheet of paper, write the same first word: *Yesterday*. Follow this with a paragraph or two recounting yesterday's events, sort of a postgame analysis.

Write whatever you want—perhaps a little description of the people you interacted with, your appointments, decisions, thoughts, feelings, high points, low points, frustrations, what you read in your Bible, what you were going to do and didn't. According to MacDonald, this exercise causes a tremendous step forward in spiritual development.

His approach didn't turn me completely off, as my visions of midday mystics had done. On the other hand, I was skeptical. *Come on,* I thought, *what could that exercise possibly do?*

Most of us, the author said, live unexamined lives. We repeat the same errors day after day. We don't learn much from the decisions we make, whether they are good or bad. We don't know why we're here or where we're going. One benefit of journaling is to force us to examine our lives.

But an even greater benefit, he said, is this: the very act of journaling—sitting down, reaching for the spiral notebook, focusing our thoughts on our life, writing for five or ten minutes—will reduce our rpms from ten thousand to five thousand.

That's just what I need, I thought.

I have a high energy level in the morning. I can't wait to get to the office to start the day's work. And once the adrenaline starts flowing, the phone starts ringing, the people start coming, I can easily stay at ten thousand rpms until I crash at night. So I decided to start journaling. What did I have to lose?

My first journal entry began, "Yesterday I said I hated the concept of journals and I had strong suspicions about anyone who has the time to journal, and I still do, but if this is what it's going to take to slow me down so I can learn to talk and walk with Christ the way I should, I'll journal."

And I do. Every day! I don't think I've ever written anything profound in my journal, but then that's not the point. The amazing thing is what happens to my rpms when I write. By the time I've finished a long paragraph recapping yesterday, my mind is off my responsibilities, I'm tuned in to what I'm doing and thinking, and my motor is slowed halfway down.

A Page of Prayer

Journaling, then, is the important first step in slowing down to pray. It gives the body a brief rest. It focuses the mind. It frees the spirit to operate, if only for a few minutes. But even though journaling may improve your life enormously, it will not in and of itself turn you into an authentic Christian. It's only a first step in the right direction.

After you have bought a spiral notebook, filled the first page and reduced your rpms by half, what's the next step? Your engine is still racing at speeds that would prove disastrous in an ordinary car.

Step two in the rpm-reduction program is one you already know about and perhaps have even started practicing. I described it in chapter four: *Write out your prayers.*

Some people tell me they don't need to schedule regular time for prayer; they pray on the run. These people are kidding themselves. Just try building a marriage on the run. You can't build a relationship that way, with God or with another person. To get to know someone, you have to slow down and spend time together.

So after journaling has reduced my rpms from ten thousand to five thousand, I flip all the way to the back of my spiral notebook and write a prayer. As with the journal, I limit my writing to one page. This keeps the exercise from overwhelming me and ensures that I do it every day. It also takes a realistic amount of time, given the other responsibilities I face daily.

Once I write out the prayer, I put the notebook on my credenza and kneel down. Not everyone is like me in this respect, but I find I pray much more effectively on my knees. I read the prayer aloud, adding other comments or concerns as I go through it.

Quiet Enough to Listen

By this time my rpms are down to five hundred, and I'm feeling really mellow. My heart is soft, and I invite the Lord to speak to me by his Spirit. I'm quiet enough to hear if he chooses to speak in a "gentle whisper" (1 Kings 19:12; the KJV term is "still small voice").

And this is step three of the rpm-reduction program: *Listen to God.* This step is so important that the rest of the book is devoted to it. Suffice it to say here that these moments in God's presence are the ones that really matter. This is where authentic Christianity emanates from—the unhurried, silent communing of God's Spirit with ours.

You can't become an authentic Christian on a diet of constant activity, even if the activity is all church related. Ministry, Christian rock concerts, weekend conferences, church committee meetings—these all may be valuable, but they are not your main source of strength. Strength comes out of solitude. Decisions that change the entire course of your life usually come out of the holy of holies.

I'll repeat what I said at the beginning of this chapter: *the archenemy of spiritual authenticity is busyness.* It's time to slow down, reflect and listen. And it is to the vitally important topic of learning to listen that we now turn.

12

The Importance
of Listening

It's an honor to be able to speak to God. We don't have to go through a priest or a saint or any other intermediary. We don't have to follow any prescribed rituals. We don't have to wait for an appointment. Anywhere, anytime, under any circumstances, we can "approach the throne of grace with confidence, so that we may receive mercy and find grace to help us in our time of need" (Hebrews 4:16).

It's ironic, though, that most of the time we think of prayer as talking to God, rarely stopping to wonder whether God might want to talk to us. But as I've studied prayer and prayed, I've sensed God saying, "If we enjoy a relationship, why are you doing all the talking? Let *me* get a word in somewhere!"

God Wants to Speak
How does God speak to us? One way is through his Word. As we read it and meditate on it, he applies it to our lives.

A familiar verse jumps off the page at us just when we need it. It seems to take on new meaning to fit our circumstances. The verse has not changed; it has always been part of God's Word. But the Holy Spirit gives it to us when it will help us the most.

Another way God speaks to us is through people. "I provide for you," he says, as a neighbor shows up with a casserole we had no time to cook or money to buy. "I care for you," he says, through the arms of a friend who understands our grief and seeks to console us. "I guide you," he says, through a counselor who points us to the path God has chosen for us.

A third way God speaks to us is through direct leadings of the Holy Spirit. This third Person of the Godhead is ready, willing and able to communicate with us. According to Scripture, he leads, rebukes, affirms, comforts and assures Christ's followers.

A lot of Christians, however, don't expect God to speak to them. By their actions you would expect that Jesus packed up and went back to heaven forty days after his resurrection and hasn't been heard from since. Though this attitude is common, it does not fit the picture of God painted throughout Scripture.

God Spoke to Israel

Scripture is full of accounts of God speaking to his children, directly and personally. God walked in the Garden of Eden "in the cool of the day" and stopped to talk with Adam and Eve (Genesis 3:8). He spoke frequently to Abraham, calling him from one place, leading him to another and promising to make of him a great nation. He talked to Moses through the burning bush, on top of Sinai and whenever Moses needed counsel in leading the children of Israel to the Promised Land. He gave Joshua military advice to enable the Israelites to conquer the fierce Canaanites. He talked with David about governing Israel and about his personal sins and struggles. In fact, all through the Old Testament God spoke and his people listened to—or chose to ignore—his words. The pattern is repeated in the New Testament.

God Spoke to the Early Church

God spoke to Saul the persecutor through a blinding light on the Damascus road. He then guided Paul the apostle as he traveled across the Roman Empire preaching the gospel. He spoke to the apostle Peter through a vision, telling him to extend Christian fellowship to a Gentile household. He spoke to the apostle John during his exile on a lonely island, showing him God's purposes in human history. Through the Holy Spirit he guided all the members of the early church as they selected leaders, provided for each other's needs and carried the good news of Jesus Christ wherever they went.

And Jesus promised that the Holy Spirit would stay with the church forever: "I will ask the Father, and he will give you another Counselor to be with you forever—the Spirit of truth. . . . I will not leave you as orphans; I will come to you" (John 14:16-18).

It makes no sense to believe that God lost his voice at the end of the first century. If the essence of Christianity is a personal relationship between the almighty God and individual human beings, it stands to reason that God still speaks to believers today. You can't build a relationship on one-way speeches. You need frequent, sustained, intimate contact between two persons, both of whom speak and both of whom listen.

A two-way conversation between a mortal human being and the infinite God would certainly be supernatural—but what's so surprising about that? The normal Christian life has a supernatural dimension. As the apostle Paul says in 2 Corinthians 5:7, "We live by faith, not by sight."

Listening to God speak to us through his Holy Spirit is not only normal; it is essential. Paul wrote, "You . . . are controlled . . . by the Spirit, if the Spirit of God lives in you. And if anyone does not have the Spirit of Christ, he does not belong to Christ" (Romans 8:9). He told believers to "live by the Spirit," to be "led by the Spirit, " to "keep in step with the Spirit" (Galatians 5).

Once a person turns his or her life over to Jesus Christ, it is no longer business as usual. Life no longer consists only of that which can be seen or smelled or felt or figured out by human logic. It includes walking by faith, and that means opening oneself to the miraculous ministry of the Holy Spirit.

Two Misguided Approaches

And yet some of us are reluctant to open ourselves to God's leadings. We may know Christians who claim to be doing this, but their approach makes us uncomfortable. They have performed a kind of intellectual lobotomy on themselves, and they expect the Holy Spirit to choose their socks in the morning and their restaurant for dinner. They claim to experience a leading an hour, a vision a day, a miracle a week.

I'm concerned that these people are so heavenly minded that they are of little earthly use. What they try to pawn off as divine leading is really a very human form of irresponsibility. I once met such a heavenly minded pastor. He was shocked to learn how much time I spend preparing each message I give. Ordinarily I put in from ten to twenty hours reading, studying, praying and writing out three drafts of each sermon. This pastor exclaimed, "You go to all that trouble? I just walk into my pulpit and expect a miracle." I was tempted to ask him if his congregation saw his sermons as miracles.

Don't get me wrong. As I explained in the chapter on mountain-moving prayer, I've seen God work life-changing miracles in the pulpit—even my pulpit! But I think it's wrong for you to put your hands in your pockets and your brains in a drawer, jump off the pinnacle and expect God to catch you because you're already on the way down.

However, some people go to the other extreme when it comes to listening for God's voice. In reaction to obvious misinterpretations and abuses of the Holy Spirit's ministry, many Christians run in the opposite direction and become antisupernaturalists.

To these modern rationalists, the Holy Spirit's promptings seem to go against human nature and conventional thought patterns. Accustomed to walking by sight, steering their own ships and making unilateral decisions, they are squeamish about letting the Holy Spirit begin his supernatural ministry in their lives. They wish the package were a little neater. They would like his ministry to be quantified and described. The Holy Spirit seems elusive and mysterious, and that unnerves them.

So when they sense a leading that might be from the Holy Spirit, they resist it. They analyze it and conclude, "It isn't logical; therefore, I won't pay attention to it." They question the Spirit's guidings, rebukes and attempts to comfort.

Other people *want* to obey the Holy Spirit, but they're just not sure how they'd know when he was really speaking. Are they hearing their own desires or God's still, small voice? Not wanting to go off the deep end, they avoid the water altogether.

All these reactions are understandable. In fact, I've often had them myself. But the results of automatically resisting supernatural leadings are usually unfortunate. People who cut themselves off from God's direction find their religious experience becoming cerebral, predictable, boring and—often—past tense.

The Spirit and Eternal Destiny

In a later chapter we will look at ways to tell if a leading is truly from the Holy Spirit. This may be an important chapter for Holy Spirit enthusiasts who seem to their rationalistic friends to lack common sense. In this chapter, however, we will look at the other side of the coin.

Why is it important to be interested in the Holy Spirit's leadings in your life?

First, *your eternal destiny is determined by how you respond to leadings from God.*

If you asked several seasoned believers how they came to personal faith in Christ, you would probably find a similar pattern in their experiences. Most would refer to the mark some Christian made on their lives. Most would tell of hearing the message of Jesus Christ. And then, in almost every case, they would mention an internal nudge that drove them into the arms of Christ.

"When I heard what Jesus Christ did for me," they might say, "I had a feeling, an inner tug to learn more, to walk a ways down that path to see what was at the end of it. It was like I was being led toward Christ."

In John 6:44 Jesus said, "No one can come to me unless the Father who sent me draws him." Who draws us to Christ? God, in the person of the Holy Spirit, draws and loves and tugs and urges and leads seekers to the cross.

If you're a Christian, you probably can remember that tug from God which led you first to the cross, where you acknowledged that Christ paid for your sin, and then to repentance, forgiveness and newness of life. The wonderful thing is, even after you're a Christian, God keeps tugging!

The Spirit and Assurance
Second, leadings from the Holy Spirit are important because *your assurance as a Christian depends in part on how you receive and respond to them.*

Sometime when you're in an airport, observe the difference between passengers who hold confirmed tickets and those who are on standby. The ones with confirmed tickets read newspapers, chat with their friends or sleep. The ones on standby hang around the ticket counter and pace back and forth. The difference is caused by the confidence factor.

If you knew that in fifteen minutes you would have to stand in judgment before the Holy God and learn your eternal destiny, what would your reaction be? Would you pace nervously? Would you say to yourself, "I don't know what God's going to say—will it be 'Welcome home, child,' or will it be 'Depart from me; I never knew you'"?

Or would you drop to your knees and worship Jesus Christ? Would you say to yourself, "I just can't wait, because I know God is going to open the door and invite me in"? Again, the difference is caused by the confidence factor.

What does this have to do with leadings? Paul says in Romans 8:16: "The Spirit himself testifies with our spirit that we are God's children." In other words, the Holy Spirit whispers and tugs and nudges and makes impressions on the spirits of true believers, and this is what he says: "Rejoice! You've trusted Christ, and now you're a member of the family. Relax! The agonizing is over; you're on the flight to heaven."

In a hundred different ways, using all kinds of leadings, the Holy Spirit comforts and communicates with believers, convincing them that they can have absolute confidence they are accepted into God's family.

That's the way to live—unafraid of death, because the Holy Spirit has assured you of where you will be beyond the grave. God promises that kind of assurance to his family members. If your experience is not like that, if you identify with the airport pacers, you probably haven't yet put your trust entirely in Christ. You may still be trying to earn your own ticket to heaven. Your anxiety can be your best friend, if it drives you into Christ's arms for assurance of God's love for you.

The Spirit and Christian Growth

The third reason leadings are important is this: *your growth as a Christian depends on receiving and responding to leadings.*

Jesus promised in John 16:13, "When he, the Spirit of truth, comes, he will guide you into all truth." The Holy Spirit will prompt you, tug at you and guide you as you read and heed the Word of God.

As believers, of course, we are responsible to obey God's entire Word. But the Bible is a big book, and we can't swallow it all at once. So God often gives us his truth one bite-sized piece at a time. This is what he did for me.

When I became a Christian at age sixteen, I sensed the Holy Spirit saying to me, "You need to understand doctrine: the difference between grace and good works as a means of getting to heaven, the meaning of faith, the identity of God, the person of Jesus Christ, the work of the Holy Spirit." So I studied and prayed and talked to friends and took courses on doctrinal issues.

A few years later, the focus changed. Now the emphasis was on character. Every time I turned around the Holy Spirit seemed to say to me, "You need to grow in sensitivity and compassion." I have a hard time being a kind, gentle, tenderhearted person; my personality is not naturally that way. And so I read and studied and memorized verses like Ephesians 4:32: "Be kind and compassionate to one another, forgiving each other, just as in Christ God forgave you."

Later, after I married, the Holy Spirit pierced my soul as

if with daggers and said, "You are not living like a godly husband; you do not treasure your wife 'as Christ loved the church and gave himself up for her' (Ephesians 5:25). Right now the most important thing for you to learn is how to be a loving husband."

In recent years the Holy Spirit has urged me to study prayer—how we can best communicate with God, and how he speaks to us. Next month, next year, he will probably lead me to focus on a different truth.

If you remain sensitive to the Holy Spirit's leadings and cooperate with them as you receive them, you can trust him to guide you into the truth and to help you grow up as a Christian. That doesn't give you license to ignore parts of Scripture and say, "Well, that's not what the Holy Spirit is emphasizing in my life right now." We're responsible for hearing the whole Word of God. Nevertheless, the Holy Spirit has a way of emphasizing different areas at different times.

The Spirit and Guidance

The fourth reason you need to be attuned to the leadings of the Holy Spirit is that *your life plans are greatly affected by how you receive and respond to God's leadings.*

You matter to God. He made you, and he knows what will fulfill you. He knows what vocation is best suited to your talents and abilities. He knows if you should marry or remain single, and if you marry, he knows which marriage partner is best suited to you. He knows what church you can flourish in. And this is what he says to you: "I want to guide your life. I know the path that will glorify me and be productive for you, and I want to put you on it. I'll do that primarily through leadings, so quiet your life and listen to me."

It is to this important subject we will now turn—how to listen for and hear the Holy Spirit as he speaks to you.

13

How to Hear God's Leadings

Hearing the Holy Spirit's leadings is vitally important to a healthy Christian life. The Spirit nudges us to accept God's offer of salvation, assures us that we are members of God's eternal family, encourages us to grow and guides us along the path God has chosen for us. But often when the Spirit tries to get through to us, he gets a busy signal.

What changes do we need to make so that when God speaks to us through his Spirit, we will be able to hear him?

The Discipline of Stillness

People who are really interested in hearing from God must pay a price: they must discipline themselves to be still before God. This is not an easy task, but it is essential. Psalm 46:10 says, "Be still, and know that I am God."

Jesus developed the discipline of stillness before God in spite of his extremely busy life. Crowds followed him wherever he went. Daily he preached and taught and healed. It was hard for him to find time alone to pray, and he had to get up long before dawn to do it. "Very early in the morning, while it was still dark, Jesus got up, left the house and went off to a solitary place, where he prayed" (Mark 1:35).

Times of stillness and solitude were important to Jesus. In those times of seclusion, he not only poured out his heart to the Father, he earnestly listened to him as well. He needed his Father's comfort, direction, affirmation and assurance. Because of the continual leadings he received from the Father, there was purpose to his steps. The people around him saw his confidence and certainty, and they were amazed "because he taught them as one who had authority" (Mark 1:22).

If Jesus were the only person mentioned in Scripture who took time to listen to the Lord, we would have a strong example to follow. But he is not alone. King David, author of many of the psalms, "went in and sat before the LORD." The prophet Isaiah, before taking on an immensely difficult commission from God, listened to God in his temple (Isaiah 6). The apostle Peter "went upon the roof to pray" at lunch time, and God talked to him there (Acts 10:9-20). Scripture is full of accounts of people who took time to hear what God had to say to them.

Strength from Solitude

God's power is available to us when we come to him in solitude, when we learn how to focus and center our hearts and be quiet before him. When we learn the discipline of stillness before God, we find that his leadings come through to us clearly, with little interference.

That is why I have made the commitment to spend from half an hour to an hour every single morning in a secluded place with the Lord. I don't do this to earn merit badges from God. I do it because I grew very tired of leading an unexamined life.

I used to try to pray and receive God's leadings on the run. But it became obvious to me that the pace of my life outstripped my capacity to analyze it. It exhausted me to be constantly doing and rarely reflecting on what I did. At the end of a day I would wonder if my work had any meaning at all.

So I developed my own disciplined approach to stillness before God. It is the only spiritual discipline I have ever really stuck with, and I am not tempted to abandon it because it has made my life so much richer.

After I reflect on the previous day and write out my prayers, my spirit is quiet and receptive. That is when I write an *L* for *listen* on a piece of paper and circle it. Then I sit quietly and simply say, "Now, Lord, I invite you to speak to me by your Holy Spirit."

The moments with God that follow are the ones that really matter. This is where authentic Christianity comes from. Not from prayers on the run, not at Christian concerts or conferences, not when I'm flying around here and there, even if I'm engaged in ministry.

No one can become an authentic Christian on a steady diet of activity. Power comes out of stillness; strength comes out of solitude. Decisions that change the entire course of your life come out of the holy of holies, your times of stillness before God.

I like my way of quieting my mind and preparing myself to hear God speak; it works well for me. But I know it won't work for everyone. Some people can't stand writing anything, let alone journals and prayers. They may prefer to talk quietly to God. Some are good at meditating without writing or saying a word. Some "come before him with joyful songs" (Psalm 100:2).

The important thing is not to follow a particular method but to find a way that works for you. Custom-design an approach that will still your racing mind and body, soften your heart and enable you to hear God's still, small voice. Then, when you are centered and focused on God, invite him to speak to you.

Questions for God

I have several questions I regularly ask God.

What's the next step in developing my character? I almost always hear from God when I ask that question, because there's always an edge he is trying to knock off my life.

What's the next step in my family—with Lynne and the kids? I get a lot of direction from God in this area too. My wife is unbelievably supportive of me, and God says, "You'd better return that. Try to serve her as enthusiastically as she serves you."

What's the next step in my ministry? I have no idea how people in ministry survive without listening to God. Most of my creative ideas for messages and programs and new directions come from my morning time with him.

Depending on your situation, you might ask:

☐ "What's the next step in my vocation?"

☐ "What direction should my dating relationship go?"
☐ "What should I do for my children?"
☐ "How should I further my education?"
☐ "How should I plan my giving?"

Whatever you ask the Lord, you will be amazed at the way he leads. Once you are quiet and tender before him, waiting to hear him speak, he will bring a verse to mind or will guide you through your thoughts and feelings. As you build the discipline of stillness into your life, you will find these quiet moments in God's presence becoming incredibly precious to you.

Answers from God

Suppose that right after reading this chapter you put down the book and quiet your spirit before God. You wait until you are focused on him, and then you say, "Speak, LORD, for your servant is listening" (1 Samuel 3:9). In the solitude and stillness, what might God say to you?

To some seekers God might say, "You've been reading Christian books and going to Christian meetings long enough. Now it's time you became a Christian. Come to me, repent of your sin and enter into a faith-oriented relationship with me."

To those who have already made that commitment he might say, "Return to me. You've been stumbling and bumbling around. It's been a long, dry summer. Let's get reacquainted! Let's have fellowship again!"

To people facing trials he might offer words of comfort: "I'm right here. I know your name, and I know your pain. I'm going to give you strength, so trust me."

To others, faithful through hardships, he might say, "I am so pleased with you! I'm glad you are being faithful even though life is difficult for you. Keep it up!"

And to still others, this message might come: "Follow my leading and take a risk. Try this new direction. Face this new challenge. Walk with me toward new horizons."

The message will be suited to the person's individual need, but the central truth is certain: we serve a God who has spoken in history, who still speaks today and who wants to speak to us.

When God Is Silent

But what if no message comes through?

Sometimes when I wait quietly for God to speak, I sense total silence from heaven. It's as if no one's home. I have felt very silly in those times. Did I ask the wrong question? Was I foolish to expect answers? Was God really listening?

After thinking about it, I've concluded that I don't need to feel upset if sometimes God chooses to remain silent. He's a living Being, not an answering machine, and he speaks when he has something to say.

Sometimes I ask my wife, "Is there anything you want to tell me that we haven't had time to sit down and talk about?" My question gives Lynne the opportunity to tell me anything she wants, but it doesn't force her to talk. Sometimes she says, "No, nothing in particular." And that's fine. More often than not, though, she does have a message for me — and so does God, when I invite him to speak.

Tuned In to God's Voice

I know that God continues to speak to his people today, and I am convinced that there are two reasons we don't hear his voice more often. The most obvious reason is that we don't listen for it. We don't schedule times of stillness that make communication possible.

Be honest with yourself. When do you turn off the TV, the radio, the CD player and listen to nothing louder than the refrigerator's hum? When do you turn off the sound track of your mind and come away from the numbers, machines, words, schemes or whatever it is that occupies your waking thoughts? When do you make yourself quiet and available to God? When do you formally invite him to speak to you?

Do you build the discipline of solitude right into your schedule? Try it! Like any new practice, it will feel awkward at first. Gradually it will become more natural, and eventually you will feel off balance if you don't make time for solitude every day.

In addition to carving out blocks of time to listen to God, do you keep your ears tuned to him each day? A friend of mine has a company car equipped with an AM-FM radio, a CD player, a phone and a mobile communication unit which he monitors at a very low decibel level when he's in the car. Often we've been riding together, talking and listening to music, when all of a sudden he'll reach down, pick up the microphone and say, "I'm here, what's up?"

With all the other noise in the car, I never hear the mobile unit's signal. But he has tuned his ear to it. He is able to carry on a conversation and listen to music without ever losing his awareness that a call may come over that unit.

It is possible to develop a similar sensitivity to the Holy Spirit's still, small voice. It is possible to be aware throughout the day, even while going about your daily work, of God's gentle promptings. That's what it means to "live by the Spirit" (Galatians 5:16).

Moment by Moment

These on-the-spot promptings are not a substitute for unhurried quiet time with God. In fact, they tend to come to me only when I regularly make time for stillness and solitude. But when they come, they're wonderful.

You're driving to a sales call, and almost out of nowhere you sense God by his Holy Spirit saying, "Aren't you glad you're my child? Aren't you glad you have a home in heaven? Aren't you glad I'm with you right now? Don't you feel safe and secure in my presence?" When you process a communication like that, the whole world seems to evaporate; your car becomes a sanctuary, and it's just you and the Lord enjoying each other. How people live without moments like that, I don't know.

Listen and Obey

The other reason we may not hear God's voice is that we don't plan to do anything about it. God speaks, we listen and nod and say, "How interesting!" But if we don't follow up on the Holy Spirit's leadings, he may see no reason to continue speaking. The next chapter is all about discerning God's voice and choosing to obey.

People who make opportunities for the Holy Spirit to

speak to them know that the Christian life is a continual adventure. It is full of surprises, thrills, challenges and mysteries. If you open your mind and heart to God's leadings, you will be amazed at what he will do. He is attempting to communicate with you more often than you know. You have no idea how much richer and fuller, how much more exciting and more effective your life will be once you make the decision to be still, to be aware and to obey God's leadings.

14

What to Do with Leadings

A few years ago, after a particularly exhausting meeting, I got into my car and drove out of the church parking lot onto the exit road. As I started down the road, out of the corner of my eye I saw someone walking toward the parking area. In that fraction of a second I received what I thought was a leading from God — to go offer some form of assistance to the person I had just passed.

My initial response was *Why?* The person didn't seem to be having any difficulty. My second response was *Why me?* I'd already done my share that day, studying, working on a sermon, counseling with people and then leading a meeting. I wanted to go home.

And so I kept driving, rationalizing my disobedience to the little leading from God. But the Holy Spirit persisted. By the time I had reached the entrance sign, I felt so restless in my spirit that I said, "I can't put up with this anymore. Disobedience is causing more stress than simply turning around and obeying, even if I'm tired and don't know why I'm supposed to do this."

So I headed back down the entrance road, pulled up alongside the person, who was still heading south, rolled my window down and awkwardly said, "Is there any way I can serve you? Could I drive you to your car?" (Our parking lot is large, and frequently people forget where they have parked.)

The woman, whom I had never seen before, gladly accepted my offer. Just as she was about to thank me and get out of the car, she said, "There was an announcement in the bulletin tonight about the need for administrative help in the church office, and I've been feeling God leading me to apply for that position. What do you think?"

We discussed the matter briefly, and then we each drove off. That night I had no idea how offering help to a person who probably didn't need it would affect my life and ministry. As it turned out, the woman joined our staff and served faithfully for almost ten years. I wonder what would have happened if I hadn't obeyed that leading.

Private Promptings

I was once attending a conference in Southern California where, for some strange reason in the middle of one afternoon, I felt I ought to attend a workshop in which I had very little interest. The workshop was in a different building, and as I was walking to it, I met a young man and started talking with him.

As we talked, I was impressed by his tender spirit, and I realized God was knitting our hearts together. Over the course of several months, we corresponded and then visited one another. Eventually he joined our church staff and built one of the most effective youth ministries in the country.

When God tells us to write to this person or make an appointment with that person or give away so much money, to start this or stop that or share the other thing, it doesn't have to make sense to us. Some of the most important decisions in my life have made no sense at all from a worldly perspective. But I have learned that I can't afford not to respond to his leadings.

One morning an elder of my church called me on the phone and said, "I had a leading to call you. Are you in trouble or anything?"

"Not that I know of," I said.

"All right," she said. "I'm just obeying the Lord. I wanted to call you and encourage you."

I was glad she called, even if neither of us knew exactly why. I never object to being encouraged, and I was glad she was obedient to the Holy Spirit. When God tells us to do something, as long as it's within the limits set by Scripture, we don't have to understand it. All we need to do is obey and trust God to use our obedience to accomplish his will.

Leadings are intensely private phenomena. You get them and I get them, but unless we share them, nobody knows what we do with them. I could have disobeyed that leading to help the woman in the parking lot, and nobody would have known. I could have ignored the feeling that I ought to attend the workshop that didn't interest me, and nobody would have written a news story about it.

In fact, if I had paid no attention to those leadings, I

would never have known what I missed. How could I know that the person in the parking lot was just the capable administrative assistant our staff needed, or that on my way to the workshop I would run into the best possible youth minister for my church?

I could tell story after story of leadings God has entrusted to me and to others. I could describe the dramatic effects of obeying God's leadings—or of ignoring them. But such stories may not be to the point. The real question is this: What are you going to do about the leadings *you* receive?

Is It Really from God?

When I raise this question, people sometimes ask me a question in return. "I believe in leadings," they say. "I am willing to obey. In fact, I often have done so. But I know that there are other spirits loose in this world, and they aren't all holy. I also know that I am capable of thinking that my own intense desires are the Holy Spirit's wishes. How can I be sure that a leading is truly from God?"

This is a valid question. The Bible warns us that Satan, the evil one, is capable of both issuing his own leadings for destructive purposes and undermining God's leadings in your life.

Paul wrote to Timothy, "The Spirit clearly says that in later times some will abandon the faith and follow deceiving spirits and things taught by demons" (1 Timothy 4:1).

These lying spirits may appear to be channels of God's power. John referred to "spirits of demons performing miraculous signs," (Revelation 16:14) and Jesus predicted that "false Christs and false prophets" would "perform great signs and miracles to deceive even the elect—if that were possible" (Matthew 24:24).

Evil spirits are not necessarily easy to distinguish from God's ministering spirits, the angels. As Paul pointed out, "Satan himself masquerades as an angel of light" (2 Corinthians 11:14). Therefore it is very important to know the origin of the leadings coming into your mind.

Adam and Eve followed a leading to increase their knowledge by eating an attractive fruit, and they plunged the human race into darkness and misery (Genesis 3). King David followed a leading to befriend a beautiful army wife, and it cost him his best general and a son (2 Samuel 11 — 12).

Who is really responsible for the murderous hatred that tears apart Protestants and Catholics in Northern Ireland, Jews and Arabs in Jerusalem, Iraqis and Iranians in the Persian Gulf, and Serbs and Croats and Muslims in Bosnia?

Who led Lee Harvey Oswald to shoot President Kennedy, or Idi Amin to exterminate many of his countrymen in Uganda, or a platoon of American GIs to massacre the women and children of My Lai? Who leads the Ku Klux Klan to throw rocks and bottles at their neighbors because their skin is darker than their own?

Who leads me to say hurtful things, to be arrogant, to color the truth? Who prompts me to care less about serving others than about my own advancement and fulfillment?

Heavenly Warfare

In Ephesians 6:10-18 Paul reminds us that there's a war going on in this universe. "Put on the full armor of God," he says, "so that you can take your stand against the devil's schemes. For our struggle is not against flesh and blood, but against the rulers, against the authorities, against the powers of this dark world and against the spiritual forces of evil in the heavenly realms" (vv. 11-12).

This war is being waged on the spiritual battlefields of our minds. As God leads people for his glory and for their benefit, Satan does everything in his power to undo God's work and undermine his activity in people's lives. Because of this spiritual war, it is possible that some of the notions that come into our heads have been authored in hell, not heaven.

There are only two ways to respond to devilish leadings: flight or fight. "Flee the evil desires of youth," Paul told the youthful Timothy (2 Timothy 2:22). "Resist the devil, and he will flee from you," James wrote (James 4:7).

But how can you be sure where a particular leading is coming from?

In 1 John 4:1 we read, "Dear friends, do not believe every spirit, but test the spirits to see whether they are from God, because many false prophets have gone out into the world." I'm going to suggest three criteria by which to test leadings you receive.

Consistent with Scripture

First, *all leadings that come from God are consistent with his Word, the Bible.*

The surest way to test the source of a leading is to check it against Scripture. As I interact with people in my church, almost every month someone tells me he is being led to be unfaithful to his wife. He thinks he is being led to the woman God chose for him, and that his marriage is a regrettable mistake—a sin, even. The only way he can do God's will, he tells me, is to repent of his sin and unite his life with the woman he should have married in the first place.

The rationalizations are often very sophisticated, but the bottom line is always the same—people want to divorce the spouses to whom they were joined in holy matrimony in order to marry others who seem more attractive. This is not a leading from God: I can say that unequivocally. Listen to what God says:

> May you rejoice in the wife of your youth. . . . May you ever be captivated by her love. Why be captivated, my son, by an adulteress? (Proverbs 5:18-20)

> [The Lord] no longer pays attention to your offerings or accepts them with pleasure from your hands. You ask, "Why?" It is because the Lord is acting as the witness between you and the wife of your youth, because you have broken faith with her, though she is your partner, the wife of your marriage covenant. . . . "I hate divorce," says the LORD God of Israel. (Malachi 2:13-14, 16)

A leading to be unfaithful to your spouse is never a leading from God. Neither is a leading to cheat on an examination, to exaggerate to a customer, to spread hurtful gossip, to deceive your parents or children, or to do anything else forbidden by Scripture.

If the leading goes against the Bible, it obviously comes from an unholy spirit. Call it Satanic and dismiss it summarily. There is no other Christian way to deal with an unscriptural leading.

Consistent with God's Gifts

On the other hand, a leading may be consistent with God's Word and still not be sent by the Holy Spirit. For example, nothing in the Bible told Jesus he should not turn stones into bread, as the devil was urging him to do. He had other reasons for refusing to do what Satan said.

If a leading is not contrary to Scripture, it's time to look at the second criterion: *God's leadings are usually consistent with the person he made you to be.*

Some people seem to think that God creates a person with certain gifts and then expects the person to excel in totally unrelated fields. I've met people who adore math and computers and do very well in those areas, but they assume God is leading them into music or theology.

Some people who love the outdoors and don't really come alive unless they're in nature nevertheless assume God is leading them toward a downtown nine-to-five office job on the thirty-fifth floor of a high-rise.

I've even met people who are uncomfortable around children and still think God is leading them to become schoolteachers.

I ask these people, "Why do you assume God's leadings would contradict who he made you to be? Why would he design you for one purpose and then ask you to fulfill another?"

Our God is purposeful. He is the master orchestrator and synthesizer of the universe. To be sure, he loves to stretch our abilities and expand our potential, and that often involves leading us along untried paths. That does not mean, however, that he ignores our gifts and inherent interests.

After all, he gave them to us in the first place so that we could serve him more effectively! Instead, he strengthens our natural abilities and builds on them.

If you sense a leading that seems completely contrary to who God made you to be, I advise you to test it very carefully. Is God asking you to do this difficult thing because there is simply no one else who will do it? Is he asking you to stretch into new areas so that your unique gifts will grow? Or is this perhaps not a God-inspired leading at all, but rather a distraction from the task God has given you to do?

The Servanthood Dimension

Third, *God's leadings usually involve servanthood.* I find that many counterfeit leadings are fairly easy to discern, because they are self-promoting or self-serving. It never fails—in late January or early February when the Midwest goes into the deep freeze, I feel a strange but compelling calling to start a church in Honolulu.

A frustrated man called me recently and said, "I've been an elder in my church for thirty years, and I've seen a lot of pastors come and go. I'd like to know why every one of them has felt a leading to leave this church when the invitation elsewhere involved more money, more benefits, a bigger staff and a larger house. No pastor has ever been led to a smaller church with a smaller salary and fewer benefits."

Over the years I've found that if a leading promises easy money and fame and perks and toys, I'd better watch out. Prosperity has ruined more people than servanthood and adversity ever will. On the other hand, I can usually sense that a leading is from the Holy Spirit when it calls me to humble myself, serve somebody, encourage somebody or give something away. Very rarely will the evil one lead us to do those kinds of things.

This is what Paul told the Ephesian elders about one of his leadings: "Now, compelled by the Spirit, I am going to Jerusalem, not knowing what will happen to me there. I only know that in every city the Holy Spirit warns me that prison and hardships are facing me" (Acts 20:22-23). Paul was not being asked to do something contrary to his gifts—all the way to Jerusalem he would be preaching the gospel and strengthening young churches. He was, however, being asked to sacrifice safety and comfort for the sake of the kingdom.

Not every leading from God will involve pain and sacrifice, but expect that quite often God's leadings will mean making gut-wrenching decisions that test the limits of your faith and make you face life's ultimate issues head-on. Many of God's leadings will require you to choose between being comfortable and building a godly character, amassing money and seeking first God's kingdom, being a winner in the world's eyes and being a winner in God's eyes.

So if a leading promises you overnight health, wealth, comfort and happiness, be cautious. God led Jesus to a cross, not a crown, and yet that cross ultimately proved to be the gateway to freedom and forgiveness for every sinner in the world. God also asks us as Jesus' followers to carry a cross. Paradoxically, in carrying that cross, we find liberty and joy and fulfillment.

Proceed with Caution

Thus we can summarize that a leading is probably from God

if it is consistent with his Word, if it is congruent with who he made you to be and if it requires some sacrifice or steps of faith. Let me add a few cautions:

☐ If a leading requires you to make a major, life-changing decision in a very short period of time, question it.

☐ If a leading requires you to go deeply in debt or place someone else in a position of awkwardness, compromise or danger, question it.

☐ If a leading requires you to shatter family relationships or important friendships, question it.

☐ If a leading creates unrest in the spirit of mature Christian friends or counselors as you share it with them, question it.

I'm not saying you should automatically reject such leadings unless they are also against Scripture, but reconsider them and treat them very carefully. Leadings from God can open the door to a fantastically fulfilling Christian adventure, but counterfeit leadings can cause unbelievable amounts of confusion, hardship, pain and trauma.

Test and Obey

I don't want to end this chapter on a negative note. It is a terrible loss when Christians are so afraid of counterfeit leadings that they close their ears to the Holy Spirit's leadings too. God wants us to test the spirits, of course, but then he wants us to step out in faith and follow him.

Some years ago I had lunch at a restaurant with a man who was not a believer. His friends had told me that he was the toughest, hardest hitting, most autocratic, hardheaded, hardhearted man they had ever met. (With a recommendation like that, I didn't bother to check with his enemies.)

Twenty minutes into the meal, I could affirm everything they had said.

We were talking about everything but important things when I felt a leading. The Holy Spirit seemed to whisper to me, "Present the simple truth of Jesus dying for sinners as clearly as you possibly can right now."

I didn't want to do that. I thought I knew for certain what his response would be. But the leading was certainly biblical. It fit my gifts, at least under other circumstances, and it was not in any way self-serving! I had a choice: would I trust God, or would I disobey this leading which clearly seemed to be from him?

I obeyed. Abruptly changing the subject, I asked, "Would you like to know how Jesus Christ takes sinners to heaven?"

"Pardon me?" said the man.

"Point of information," I said. "Would you like to know how Jesus Christ forgives sinners and takes them to heaven?"

"I guess so," he reluctantly agreed.

So, over dessert, I explained the plan of salvation as plainly and as briefly as I knew how. He asked a few questions. We finished lunch, and I went back to work feeling slightly embarrassed.

Two or three days later I almost fell off my chair when the man called me. He said, "Do you know what I did after our lunch together? I went into my bedroom, got on my knees and said, 'I'm a sinner in need of a Savior.'"

That man became a strong Christian. His spirit mellowed, and he became one of my closest friends. We had seven wonderful years of fellowship together before he went to be with the Lord. And it all can be traced back to a leading.

When you begin to listen for God's leadings, you often won't know why he is asking you to do something. He will lead you down paths through unknown territory, sometimes for no other reason than to teach you to trust him. Remember, the Christian walk is based on faith, not sight (2 Corinthians 5:7), and "without faith it is impossible to please God" (Hebrews 11:6).

For a truly dynamic, authentic, exciting Christian life, listen for the Holy Spirit's leadings. Test them. And then obey them. Roll the spiritual dice. Take a faith gamble. Give it a shot. Cooperate with God. Say yes to him, even if it seems risky or illogical. You will be amazed at what God will do.

15

Living in God's Presence

The purpose of prayer is not simply to draw up one's requests and praises and present them in an acceptable fashion to God. It is not simply to become aware of God's answers and guidance. God doesn't instruct us to pray without ceasing just so he can easily send us revised directions whenever needed.

The purpose of prayer goes deeper than that. Prayer is a way to maintain constant communion with God the Father and God the Son through God the Holy Spirit. It is the means of living out the intense relationship Jesus described in John 15:5-8 (NRSV):

I am the vine, you are the branches. Those who abide in me and I in them bear much fruit, because apart from me you can do nothing. Whoever does not abide in me is thrown away like a branch and withers; such branches are gathered, thrown into the fire, and burned. If you abide in me, and my words abide in you, ask for whatever you wish, and it will be done for you. My Father is glorified by this, that you bear much fruit, and become my disciples.

A book about prayer would be incomplete without mention of God's abiding presence with his followers. Prayer and God's presence are two sides of the same coin. Awareness of God's presence comes as the result of taking time to speak and listen to him through prayer; conversely, the power of prayer is unleashed in the lives of those who spend time in God's presence.

Forgiver, Lord and Friend

Too many Christians know a lot about God but rarely or never experience his presence in their lives. I was raised in a denomination that stresses God's transcendence. We thought of God in lofty and exalted terms, as well we should, but we overemphasized that side of him. He seemed lifted up far above his creatures and worshipers, and the distance between us often seemed unbridgeable.

I knew what it meant to fear God, and I understood the importance of serving him. I expected one day to stand under his judgment, and I believed it was my duty to obey his commandments. But one thing was sorely lacking in my Christian experience: any real understanding of the close relationship God wishes to have with his children.

In college I met a professor who amazed me. He would sometimes talk about his relationship with Jesus Christ as though he had just had lunch with him. He seemed to be able to relate to Jesus as to a friend or brother, having relaxed conversations with him.

I couldn't understand that type of relationship with the "immortal, invisible, God only wise, in light inaccessible hid from our eyes"—but I wanted it. And so I started hanging around the professor after class until one day I got up the courage to ask, "How do you seem to know Christ in a way that I don't?"

His answer clicked in my mind: "Maybe you understand Jesus only as the forgiver of your sins."

The professor was right. A few years earlier I had admitted my sinfulness and recognized my need for a Savior. I had bowed the knee to Christ, and he had cleansed me. Grateful for his grace in my life, I had been praying, "O Lord, thank you for dying on the cross to forgive my sins."

Besides relating to Jesus as forgiver, I also related to him as Lord of my life. But I didn't yet understand the whole dimension of relating to him as he asked us to in John 15:15: "I no longer call you servants, because a servant does not know his master's business. Instead, I have called you friends, for everything that I learned from my Father I have made known to you."

Practicing the Presence

"If Jesus were to explain this verse to you personally," the professor told me, "this is what he might say: 'I want to relate to you as your forgiver and Lord, but I also want to be your friend. I want our conversations to bring you comfort. I'd like our dialogues to have some give-and-take. I'd like for you to think about me during your day. I want you to know you're never alone, to feel that wherever you go and whatever you do, there's a companion by your side. I want you to discover my presence in your daily life.' "

Brother Lawrence, a cook in a seventeenth-century French monastery, gave the world a phrase that well describes such a deep friendship with Jesus: *the practice of the presence of God.* As this humble monk washed dishes and served food to his brothers, he communed with God, and the glow of God's presence gave his menial kitchen duties richness and significance.

I discovered Brother Lawrence's book at about the time my professor was challenging me to get acquainted with Jesus as a friend; and from the monk's book and my professor's teachings and example, I gradually became aware of God's presence in my own life. From Brother Lawrence I learned that in my car, on the job, at home, while working out, while helping somebody move, while lying in bed at night, anytime, anywhere, under any circumstances, I could commune meaningfully with the Lord. God was near me and wanted to enjoy a friendship with me through his Son, Jesus.

God's Presence in History

Going to the Bible, I discovered that throughout recorded history God has taken pains to let his people know of his presence among them.

After leading the Israelites out of Egypt and into the desert, God knew they would feel frightened and alone. Responsible for their children and livestock, they were camping in a place with wild animals, little food and practically no water. They had no armies and no walls to protect them from enemy attack. They didn't even know the way to the Promised Land.

In their heads, they knew they were God's people and he had promised to protect them. But it was hard to feel his presence. And so God, wanting to convince them that he was with them wherever they went, gave them a visible sign of his presence. "By day the LORD went ahead of them in a pillar of cloud to guide them on their way and by night in a pillar of fire to give them light" (Exodus 13:21).

If ever the people began to wonder if their journey was headed in the right direction, all they had to do was look up and see the pillar of cloud. If ever they grew frightened of animals or enemies that might be stalking them by night, all they had to do was look at the pillar of fire casting its glow over the whole camp. God made sure that they could feel his presence in their midst.

The Old Testament tells of many ways God let his people know he was among them: through the tabernacle that accompanied Israel on its journeys; through his Shekinah glory that rested over the ark in the temple; through a whole succession of prophets that spoke his word to the people. But the fullness of God's presence was yet to come.

God with Us

The New Testament begins with God offering us his presence in the person of Jesus Christ, his Son.

The promised baby was to be called *Immanuel* "God with us" (Matthew 1:23). John explains the significance of Jesus' birth: "The Word became flesh and made his dwelling among us" (John 1:14). Theologians call this the *incarnation* — God putting on human flesh and actually living with his people.

God's presence on earth through Jesus Christ was not some otherworldly, mystical phenomenon. It was not something that could be discerned only by priests, prophets or intellectuals. John emphasized the physical reality of the incarnation:

> That which was from the beginning, which we have *heard*, which we have *seen* with our eyes, which we have looked at and our hands have *touched*—this we proclaim concerning the Word of life. The life appeared; we have seen it and testify to it, and we proclaim to you the eternal life, which was with the Father and has appeared to us." (1 John 1:1-2)

God's presence through Jesus was powerful. It transformed ordinary, sinful people into apostles who "turned the world upside down" (Acts 17:6 KJV). Even unbelieving leaders recognized what it was that made the difference in these men: "When they saw the courage of Peter and John and realized that they were unschooled, ordinary men, they were astonished and they took note that these men had been with Jesus" (Acts 4:13).

Christ in You

But as powerful as God's presence in Christ was, it still lacked something. Jesus' ministry on earth lasted only about three years. He never left Palestine. Only a relatively small number of people ever met him personally. The vast majority of people who have lived on earth have never come in direct contact with him. That is why Jesus promised his disciples, "I will ask the Father, and he will give you another Counselor to be with you forever—the Spirit of truth" (John 14:16-17).

Shortly after Jesus ascended to the Father, that promise

was fulfilled. On the day of Pentecost God sent the Holy Spirit to take up permanent residence in the lives of believers.

Ever since Pentecost, all believers have a strong sign of God's presence with them. The moment you bow to Christ and become his, God cleanses you of your sin and simultaneously fills you with his Holy Spirit. The indwelling Spirit then begins broadcasting to your own spirit a nonstop signal proclaiming God's presence in your life. Over a period of time, you grow to realize you are never alone. God's presence is real. You can feel it. It's with you wherever you go.

When you practice being aware of God's presence, you pick up his signals all through the day. At work, at home, in your car or wherever you are, you begin to dialogue with the Lord. You share your heart with him, and you know he's listening. It has nothing to do with being in a church building or on your knees. It has to do with God's presence in and around you—"Christ in you, the hope of glory" (Colossians 1:27).

Being aware of God's presence is a great feeling that brings many benefits.

A Faithful Friend
First, when you increase your awareness of God's presence, you gain *divine companionship.*

You don't have to live long to discover that God created people to thrive on companionship. Children love to play with friends, and adolescents enjoy socializing. Adults maintain relationships with friends and colleagues and make lifetime commitments to a spouse and children.

No matter how many or how deep your friendships, however, at some point you begin to realize that human companionship is not enough. Even the best of friends can't be around you all the time. They move away, fade away or die. They don't always understand what you are going through. They aren't always faithful and dependable. If you try to meet all your companionship needs through human beings, you are doomed to perpetual, unfulfilled yearnings.

But God does not expect us to have only human friends. Proverbs 18:24 says, "There is a friend who sticks closer than a brother." Hebrews 4:15 tells us that Jesus, having been "tempted in every way, just as we are," understands us completely. Psalm 121:3 assures us that our divine friend is always available to us: "He who watches over you will not slumber."

Your heavenly Friend always listens. He freely communicates with you without barriers. When he expresses affection, he means it. He is patient with your immaturity, he forgives you when you wrong him, and he stays committed to you even when you ignore him for long periods of time. He is always faithful.

A Basis for Trust

A second benefit that comes from cultivating a relationship with Christ and living in his presence is *supernatural confidence.*

Companionship is wonderful. Even more wonderful is realizing who your closest companion is—God almighty, the Creator and Sustainer of the universe, able to empower you to face anything that comes your way.

When I was a young teenager learning to sail my dad's sailboat, I'd often take a junior-high-age friend out on Lake

Michigan. If I saw a threatening cloud formation coming our way, however, or if the winds began feeling a bit strong, I'd quickly take the sails down and head for the shore. It was nice having a pal with me. The companionship was pleasant. But in a storm, my inexperienced crew would be no good to me at all.

Other times my dad and I would sail together. Again I'd take the helm, but with Dad in the boat I eagerly looked for cloud formations and heavy winds. My dad had sailed across the Atlantic Ocean, had survived five days of hurricane and was able to handle anything Lake Michigan could throw at us. With him on board, I had both companionship and confidence.

As you enjoy God's presence in your life, you become increasingly aware of your companion's identity and power and character. Nothing is too difficult for God to handle. There are no limits to his power. Life can't throw anything at you that you can't handle with God.

You may be experiencing clear sailing right now. Having the all-powerful God as your companion may not seem very important. But I'll guarantee you that your life will not be free of storms — nobody's is. Between today and the day you die, you are going to have your share of heartbreak, disappointment, trial and tragedy. With God's presence in your life, you will be able to face these storms with confidence.

Love One Another

A third benefit of practicing the presence of God is *increased compassion for other human beings.*

The more time you spend with Christ, the more you begin

to act like him. People matter to Jesus, and what matters to him matters to his followers. His concern and compassion begin to rub off on you.

Look at what happened to the apostle John. At one point he wanted to destroy a whole city because some of its residents didn't want Jesus to stay there (Luke 9:54). After a lifetime in God's presence, John wrote, "Whoever does not love does not know God, because God is love" (1 John 4:8).

Or look at Peter, the apostle who, even after Pentecost, couldn't bear to associate with certain people (Galatians 2:11-14). In his famous "ladder" of Christian virtues, he shows how Christlike character develops: "Add to your faith goodness; and to goodness, knowledge; and to knowledge, self-control; and to self-control, perseverance; and to perseverance, godliness; and to godliness, brotherly kindness; and to brotherly kindness, love" (2 Peter 1:5-7). Through his lifelong association with Christ, Peter came to value brotherly kindness and love. He knew that it is God who helps us grow in "brotherly kindness" and at the same time makes us aware of his presence through the compassion and love of other Christians.

Recently I traveled many miles from my home to speak at a conference. Just as I was leaving my hotel room, the phone rang. It was a Christian brother from my hometown. He had tracked me down long distance just to say, "I want you to remember that whatever you're doing today, God is with you and so am I. I'm standing behind you and praying for you."

Through my friend's caring, I felt God's presence all

through the conference. And I knew that my friend was able to minister to me because God was present in his life too.

That's one way Christ is building his kingdom — by instilling his compassion in the hearts of all his followers, who then minister to each other and to the whole world. In the Old Testament, God was present in his temple. Since Pentecost, *we* have become his temple (1 Corinthians 3:16), and our concern for others helps them understand and feel God's presence.

Enjoy Him Forever

And that brings us back to the Lord's Prayer: "Thy kingdom come, thy will be done on earth as it is in heaven." What is God's will?

☐ That we believe in his love and power.

☐ That we come to him in sincerity and trust.

☐ That we clear away barriers between us, including preoccupation and excessive busyness

☐ That we listen for his still, small voice and obey it when we hear it

☐ That we live in his presence and enjoy him forever

Prayer is the way to turn dry theological descriptions into warm, living, personal realities. When we live in constant communion with God, our needs are met, our faith increases, our love expands. We begin to feel God's peace in our hearts, and we spontaneously worship him.

With the heavenly beings described in Revelation we cry out, "Worthy is the Lamb, who was slain, to receive power and wealth and wisdom and strength and honor and glory and praise! . . . To him who sits on the throne and to the

Lamb be praise and honor and glory and power, for ever and ever!" (5:12-13).

I'm enjoying God these days. He answers my prayers. He empowers me. He gives me insights from his Word. He guides my life. He gives me loving relationships. He has wonderful things in store for me.

My life with God is a constant adventure, and it all begins with prayer. Regular prayer, early in the morning, alone with him. Prayer that listens as well as speaks.

You too can enjoy God, as he created you to do. "Be joyful always; pray continually; give thanks in all circumstances, for this is God's will for you in Christ Jesus" (1 Thessalonians 5:16-17). You can feel his companionship, his capability, his compassion. He invites you to a more abundant life right now.

You are too busy not to say yes!

Questions for Reflection and Discussion

Chapter 1: God's Presence, God's Power

1. What difference does prayer make in your life?

2. How can prayer sometimes seem to impose on our individuality?

3. How do you respond to Bill Hybels's statement: *"The most intimate communion with God comes only through prayer"* (p. 10)?

4. What draws you to prayer?

5. What causes you to resist praying?

6. What is the relationship between prayer and God's power? How does this concept relate to Romans 8:26?

7. List some of the underlying questions you have concerning prayer.

8. As you begin to study this book, try to define prayer in your own words. How would you like to see your communication with God improve as you study this book?

Chapter 2: God Is Willing

1. Do you feel comfortable or uncomfortable going to God with your problems? Explain.

2. How does Bill Hybels's interpretation of the story of the widow and the judge (Luke 18:2-8) affect your attitude toward prayer?

3. What factors cause you to think that God is unwilling to respond to your prayers?

4. After reading this chapter, what makes you think that God is naturally generous?

5. When do you have a hard time accepting God's gifts to you? Why?

6. When you think of God's generosity, how often do your thoughts center on material blessings? Why?

7. What parallels can you draw between God's generosity to us and parents' generosity to their children?

Chapter 3: God Is Able

1. Do you bring your deepest needs to God every day? Why or

why not?

2. While some Christians believe God is willing to answer prayer, they inwardly question God's ability to do so. What would cause Christians to question God's ability?

3. Are there any factors that keep God from working his will in the world?

4. How can an inadequate view of God affect our prayer lives?

5. In the depths of your heart, do you believe God has the power to solve your problems? Explain.

6. Is it easier for you to go to God with small prayer requests or major requests? Explain.

7. Do you think that first-century Christians were more inclined to believe in God's power than Christians are today? Explain.

8. What is the relationship between prayer and faith? Read Hebrews 11:1, 8-18. How should faith affect the content of our prayers?

9. How could you make your prayers more sincere?

Chapter 4: Heart-Building Habits

1. How do you respond to Bill Hybels's statement: "Our spirits, like our bodies, have requirements for health and growth"?

2. Name some habits that contribute to spiritual health. Are these habits part of your life?

3. What are the warning signs of a straitjacket approach to discipline?

4. Why shouldn't we just go with the spiritual flow?

5. Are you a list maker or a free spirit? How has this affected your prayer life?

6. What decision needs to be made by everyone who is serious about growing a strong prayer life?

7. List Jesus' four prayer principles as laid out for the disciples in Matthew 6:5-13.

Chapter 5: Praying Like Jesus

1. What priority did Jesus place on prayer? How do we know this?

2. What priority do you place on prayer? How do you show this?

3. What are the advantages of seeking out a private location for

prayer?

4. How might creating a special atmosphere for your daily prayer time improve your talks with God?

5. How can you benefit from writing out your prayers?

6. Do you feel that a written prayer has disadvantages? Explain.

7. How sincere are you in your prayers? How much of your prayer life consists of empty, shallow phrases?

8. How can you avoid the habit of using meaningless repetition in prayer?

9. Is it easier for you to pray in general terms rather than specific terms? Explain.

Chapter 6: A Pattern for Prayer

1. What are the characteristics of an imbalanced prayer life?

2. Do you see the need to establish a prayer routine? Explain.

3. Bill Hybels uses the acrostic ACTS (adoration, confession, thanksgiving and supplication) to introduce us to a balanced prayer life. Which elements come easiest for you? Which elements do you most often omit?

4. Why is it good to start your prayers with adoration?

5. Why do you think adoration is so often omitted from our prayer lives?

6. How do you adore God?

7. What are some benefits of confession?

8. What changes occur in your life when you deal with sin in specific terms?

9. What is the difference between being grateful and expressing thanks to God? Why does God ask us to express thanks?

10. What categories do your prayer requests fall under? Which category gets the most attention?

Chapter 7: Mountain-Moving Prayer

1. How do you usually respond to difficulties in life?

2. In your prayers, how much of your time is spent focusing on your problems compared with the amount of time you spend focusing on God?

3. What keeps us from focusing our prayers more on God?

4. How does our focus on God change the way we see ourselves?

5. In what ways can we focus more on God in our prayer lives?

6. Are any "immovable mountains" causing you to doubt God's power or care? Explain.

7. Do you think there are mountains that God allows to remain? How does that affect your prayers?

Chapter 8: The Hurt of Unanswered Prayer

1. What difficulties do you have with unanswered prayer?

2. Can you name some inappropriate prayer requests you have made? What are some examples of inappropriate prayer requests we might make without even realizing it?

3. Why would God delay a prayer request?

4. How have you coped with the problem of unanswered prayer in the past?

5. Can you recall instances where the timing of your prayer request was wrong?

6. What are the motives behind your prayer requests?

7. How does our living in an "instant" society affect our prayer lives?

8. If some of your prayers don't seem to fit into the "no. . . slow . . . grow" categories, what other reasons might there be for unanswered prayer?

Chapter 9: Prayer Busters

1. What most motivates you to develop your prayer life?

2. What most hinders the development of your prayer life?

3. What are some "prayer busters" Bill Hybels identifies in this chapter? Can you identify some additional prayer busters?

4. How can unresolved relational conflict affect our prayer lives?

5. Can you recall some selfish prayer requests? Explain.

6. In what ways can we try to manipulate God by offering self-serving prayers?

7. Do you have trouble remembering to pray for Christians around the world? Why do we often have trouble praying for those whom we do not know personally?

8. Are there worthy activities you substitute for prayer? What are they? Why do you do this?

9. If your prayers aren't answered, do you think it is always your fault?

10. Consider the story of Job. Was Job's misfortune his own fault? Is God's first concern always to answer prayer?

Chapter 10: Cooling Off on Prayer

1. What was prayer like for you when you first got serious about praying? Have you ever experienced a cooling-off period in your prayer life?

2. Bill Hybels says, "One reason we stop praying or let our prayer lives fade is that we are too comfortable." Do you agree? Have you ever been too comfortable to pray?

3. Have you ever been driven to prayer because of serious problems you were facing? Did you continue to pray after the problems were solved?

4. Have you put a time and place for prayer in your daily schedule? When and where do you pray?

5. Has guilt ever kept you from praying? At the time, did you realize how your sin was affecting your time with God?

6. What kinds of cheating were going on in Malachi's day? How do we cheat in those categories today?

7. How can we break down the guilt barrier and restore our relationship with God?

8. How long should we persist in praying for apparently hopeless cases?

Chapter 11: Slowing Down to Pray

1. Make a list of the activities that filled your time during the past week. Do you feel that you are using your time well? Or are you overcommitted?

2. Do you truly believe that prayer is a profitable use of your time? Explain.

3. What does Bill Hybels mean by "authentic Christianity"?

4. Where does God's still, small voice fit into your hectic schedule?

5. What are some of the benefits of journaling?

6. If you have tried to journal in the past, what difficulties or benefits have you encountered?

7. Do you feel that the act of writing out your prayers would be helpful? restrictive? Explain.

8. What would keep you from writing out your prayers? How could you overcome these obstacles?

Chapter 12: The Importance of Listening

1. Does God speak to you? If so, how?

2. Do you think of prayer primarily as you talking to God, or as God talking to you? Explain.

3. What reasons does Bill Hybels give for listening to God? Do you have any additional reasons?

4. What part does listening to God play in your prayer life?

5. Do you believe listening to God can be carried to extremes? What are some of the misguided approaches Hybels lists? What other extremes would you consider dangerous?

6. Why is it important to be interested in the Holy Spirit's leading in your life?

7. What is the relationship between Christian growth and responding to God's leading?

8. Why is it important to be interested in the Holy Spirit's leading in your life?

Chapter 13: How to Hear God's Leadings

1. What factors keep us from hearing God's voice?

2. What are some benefits that come from the discipline of solitude?

3. How can solitude become intimidating to you?

4. How much time do you set aside in your prayer life to allow God to speak to you?

5. Why do you feel that Christians fail to hear God's voice more often?

6. How could you better organize your prayer time to give God more opportunities to speak to you?

7. What is your reaction when you listen for God's voice but get no response?

Chapter 14: What to Do with Leadings

1. Why are we often reluctant to respond when we receive a leading from God?

2. How can we be sure that a leading is from God? Could it be our own desires? a temptation from Satan? How can we know the difference?

3. How do you usually respond to the leadings you receive from God?

4. Have you ever responded to a leading that turned out to be false? What was the result?

5. What part does the Bible play in relationship to leadings from God?

6. Do you think God would lead us into an area where we are not gifted? Explain.

7. Has God more often led you to serve others or to be served? Explain.

8. What cautions must we exercise in trying to discern God's promptings in our lives?

9. When we listen for God's leadings, do we need to know why God is asking us to do something? Explain.

10. How do you feel when you don't feel led by God?

Chapter 15: Living in God's Presence

1. What is the relationship between prayer and living in the presence of God?

2. Is it easier for you to speak with God from a rational or an experiential perspective? Explain.

3. How has God revealed his presence throughout history?

4. Does God reveal his presence to us today? If so, how is this presence different from God's presence in Bible times? How is it similar?

5. How can we practice the presence of God in our lives?

6. What benefits come from practicing the presence of God?

7. What would it take to transform the times you wash dishes or mow the lawn into an audience with God?

8. What is the most important insight you have gained from your study of prayer?

A Guide for Private or Group Prayer

Adoration: Entering Holy Space

Read or sing one of these psalms of praise, or another of your
choosing (such as Psalm 8; 19; 23; 46; 100; 148; Luke 1:46-55, 68-79;
Ephesians 1:3-14).

> Come, let us sing for joy to the LORD;
>   let us shout aloud to the Rock of our salvation.
> Let us come before him with tanksgiving
>   and extol him with music and song.
> For the LORD is the great God,
>   the great King above all gods.
> In his hand are the depths of the earth,
>   and the moutain peaks belong to him.
> The sea is his, for he made it,
>   and his hands formed the dry land.
>
> Come, let us bow down in worship,
>   let us kneel before the LORD our Maker;
> for he is our God
>   and we are the people of his pasture,
> the flock under his care.
> (Psalm 95)

> Holy, holy, holy
> is the Lord God Almighty,
> who was, and is, and is to come. . . .

> You are worthy, our Lord and God,
>   to receive glory and honor and power,
> for you created all things,

and by your will they were created
and have their being.

Worthy is the Lamb, who was slain,
to receive power and wealth and wisdom and strength
and honor and glory and praise! . . .

To him who sits on the throne and to the Lamb
be praise and honor and glory and power,
for ever and ever!
(Revelation 4:8, 11; 5:12-13)

I worship you and praise you because you are . . .

Confession: Naming Our Faults

"If we confess our sins, he is faithful and just and will forgive us our sins
and purify us from all unrighteousness" (1 John 1:9).

I confess that I . . .
I need your forgiveness for the sin of . . .
Please give me your strength
  to forsake that sin
  to make restitution by . . .
  to accept your forgiveness and the new life you give me

I am in Christ!
I am a new creation!
The old has gone,
the new has come!
(see 2 Corinthians 5:17)

Thanksgiving: Expressing Gratitude

"Give thanks in all circumstances, for this is God's will for you in
Christ Jesus" (1 Thessalonians 5:18).

I praise you and I thank you
  for answered prayers . . .

for spiritual blessings . . .
for relational blessings . . .
for material blessings . . .
for . . .

Praise be to the LORD,
   for he has heard my cry for mercy.
The LORD is my strength and my shield;
   my heart trusts in him, and I am helped.
My heart leaps for joy
   and I will give thanks to him in song.
(Psalm 28:6-7)

Supplication: Asking for Help
"Do not be anxious about anything, but in everything, by prayer and petition, with thanksgiving, present your requests to God" (Philippians 4:6).

Here are my requests
   for other people —family, friends, acquaintances, colleagues, people in my church, people in the news . . .
   for myself—my work, my character, my health, my joys and sorrows . . .
   for . . .

"Cast all your anxiety on him because he cares for you" (1 Peter 5:7).

Glory be to the Father, and to the Son, and to the Holy Spirit.
As it was in the beginning, is now and ever shall be,
   world without end,
Amen.